DED

For my father Yann Fouéré

RECLAIMING
FATHER

BY

BENIG MAUGER

Soul
Connections

Published by Soul Connections, 69, Cowper Rd. Rathmines, Dublin 6. Ireland. www.soul-connections.com

ISBN 0-9547012-0-8

CONTENTS

ACKNOWLEDGEMENTS

Although I have gestated and given birth to this book, there were many 'fathers' involved in its conception. I would like to thank the following.

First of all my thanks go to all the men and women who have shared with me the joys and pains of loving and living and without whom the book would not have been written. I thank you for affording me the privilege to be present at your births, both physical and spiritual.

Particular thanks to those fathers, sons and lovers who shared their experiences with me: Jim Dempsey, Jeff Colley, John Fouere and David Heap all made valuable contributions. Special thanks to Tony Colley whose generosity of spirit enabled this book to be written in it's present form.

To Kieran McKeown who encouraged me in the beginning, and to Jim Fitzgerald who generously offered his knowledge and wisdom.

To Ludwig Janus of the ISPPM and to Mitch Elliot for offering me the opportunity to talk about this work in its formative time and receive valuable feedback from my colleagues in the Irish Psychological Association. Thanks also to IIPPS (Irish Institute for Psycho-Social Studies) for providing relevant information from Irish history.

To Jonathan Williams whose sensitive and perceptive editing and advice with earlier drafts set me on course.

To Brian Scott McCarthy who read some of the text and whose advice, friendship and encouragement remains invaluable.

To Brenda O'Hanlon for her encouragement and efficient editing of the manuscript, and to Paul McDaid for his talented and beautiful work in providing the book with its cover.

To Maura Lundberg for first drawing my attention to the 'spirit' that became this book, and to Paddy Mc Mahon for his unending support and encouragement through difficult times. To Gillian Doyle for being there and for proof reading at the eleventh hour.

To my friends and colleagues who helped in various ways and to my family who kept the home fires burning.

To my soul mate Bruce DiGiovanni who read and reread the text and offered invaluable help, suggestions and encouragement, and who continues to sustain me.

And finally, to my own birthplace and soul home, Connemara, where this book was written and which continues to inspire me.

INTRODUCTION

"We search this world for the great untying
Of what was wed to us at birth
And gets undone at dying'

RUMI

My last book Songs from the *Womb-Healing the Wounded Mother* (Collins, 1998) dealt mainly with the experience of giving birth and of being born. This necessarily emphasized the mother. Influenced by concerns about the soul wounds caused by the way births are managed in today's modern technology-dominated world, my aim was to highlight the spiritual and psychological dimension of childbirth and the powerful formative impact that the birth process has on our lives. The father, apart from contributing his seed, would on the surface, appear to have only a very small part to play.

Over the past few years, men have approached me at my lectures and workshops and asked 'What about the father?' When *Songs from the Womb* was published I got a similar reaction even though many men read the book and found something of value for them in it, it became clear to me that I needed to write more specifically about men as fathers.

Books have been published on the topic of fatherhood, however little has been written about men and childbirth. Nor about men as partners to pregnant and birthing women. As a natural follow on to *Songs from the Womb*, I felt strongly that something needed to be written about the importance that men have, both as partners of women giving birth, and as fathers of their children.

Mothers generally have been highlighted in the whole process of parenting, often at the expense of the father, perhaps giving the impression that he is not important. This is not so. The seminal role that the father plays in the life of his children needs to be addressed and acknowledged, particularly in today's social climate. From a psychological and spiritual perspective, the father is a complement to the mother. He is the other half of a whole. He forms his child both physically and psychologically. His influence, along with that of the child's mother, determines by and large, that child's development into adult life.

At the time this book was gestating in me I was meeting both in my personal life and in the context of my work, men who had experienced the loss of their fathers. Many of these were divorced or separated fathers. These relationships led me to explore the inner landscape of loss, particularly father loss. As I did so I learnt much about fathers and what they stand for in our psyches. I explored my own inner father and how my experience of being fathered influenced how I related to my partners. The book grew with me so that I was soon exploring the landscape of love in intimate relationships between men and women.

When the suggestion of writing this book first came up, I balked at the idea, feeling I had no right to portray a world I had not and could never inhabit. 'How can I, a woman, write about a man's experience?' I wailed to a friend over lunch one day. My friend suggested that I was overly concerned with gender and he reminded me that as a woman, I possessed an inner man, my *animus*. In Jungian psychological language this refers to the male side of my personality. Conversely, men have an *anima*, a female side. These are soul images, and they are derived from our earliest childhood experiences of the male and female, as well as collective mythological images. These images inform our thinking and our behaviour, particularly in relation to the opposite sex. Much more about this will be said later on in the book.

Shrugging off my discomfort at the notion of writing a book about men as fathers, my friend suggested I eat up and get on with it. 'Haven't you lots of experience of working with men during childbirth?' he said. He was right.

Working with couples in childbirth is only one aspect of my work. The bigger part is concerned, as any therapist's is, with easing the soul pain of other human beings on the same journey as myself. Men and women who seek to understand and heal their soul wounds through depth psychological work.

I say this because I do not want to give the impression that this book is only for and about parents and men who are fathers. It is also about relationships, particularly intimate relationships between men and women. In particular, it is about the influence that the father and the masculine energy has on the development of personality. In this regard, in an attempt to understand men's psychological makeup, this book looks in greater detail at the formative influence that fathers have on the psychological development of their sons.

The book addresses 'the father' on more than the personal level. As a Jungian psychotherapist, I see father as an archetypal masculine force, which, like the archetypal feminine, is present in us all, and is not gender related. My 'animus' therefore, could be described as my inner man. He will have been formed through my experience of my father, and to a lesser extent my brothers and all the males in my extended family. My image of the masculine or the father will act as a soul model. In this respect, the book looks in detail at the masculine spirit in women as well as men. And since this masculine is handed down to us through our fathers, it is necessary to look at the formative influence a father has on his children.

Today, at a time of great social and psychological unrest caused by changes in traditional male/female roles, improved communication between the sexes has assumed paramount importance. As I write, at the dawn of the new millennium, not only are increasing numbers of young men taking their own lives, fathers are in danger of becoming redundant. This may seem like a dramatic thing to say, but the facts are grim. As a direct result of the huge divorce rate, and the increase in the number of one-parent families headed by women, fathers are becoming more and more marginalised. This fact has huge implications for children. It also has implications for relationships between men and women.

In today's climate it is easy for fathers to feel devalued. Often deprived of their homes and sometimes their children, many divorced and separated fathers take refuge in silence. Silence because there is often no place to go to express the pain and disempowerment of losing your family and your home. It is not that there are no therapeutic structures in place, it is that men by and large do not use them. Society is so structured as to make it harder for men to admit they need psychological support. Many hurt men simply draw down the shutters on life and on love.

I think that feminism has led to a corresponding need for a men's movement. Men are becoming emasculated like never before as their traditional roles and even their biological function is being questioned. With modern fertility technology, women can now have babies without the active presence of men. Although assisted reproduction has very positive aspects, I believe that unwittingly, it, along with other factors, very subtly undermines the power of the masculine. It perhaps gives the impression that fathers are not important and that their formative influence on their children is negligible.

English writer and social researcher Rosalind Coward, author of many books on feminism, wonders whether in expounding the principles of feminism women were embracing a patriarchal system. She writes this because in her research she found that despite feminism, the traditional expectations of the family and the woman's role within it still remain virtually unchanged. Despite the achievements of feminism and modern technological advances, there has been a widespread psychological retreat into traditional values. People by and large want the traditional things such as marriage, home and children. This being the case, it is important to distinguish between masculinity or the masculine, and patriarchy. Patriarchy represents a power structure that undermines women and the feminine. Masculinity does not imply 'power over' anyone or anything. The masculine is the complement to the feminine; both are necessary components of human life. And both need to be empowered.

We are all born with an innate expectation of being mothered and fathered, and with an inherited idea of what a mother and a father are. Psychologically speaking, all children need to regard their father as a powerful figure. However, as Jungian analyst and author Robert Bly puts it, the *King* is dead, meaning that children today do not inherit a powerful father image. Instead they inherit a weakened father. The king is an archetype, an aspect of our universal image of the masculine. It and other archetypal images inform us in the way we think, feel and behave. Using the imagery of the king is Bly's way of addressing every child's need to connect with the strength making qualities of the archetypal father. The king symbolises our strength and our ability to fight for our needs and integrity. But, as Bly explains, the king can be killed off early on in our childhoods through dysfunctionality, traumatic circumstances, abuse and so on. Or we may have inherited a weak image of the father, or we may have lost him or not known him at all. When this happens, it means that the child's image is sacrificed in favour of a dysfunctional father and so the inner king dies in the son or daughter. If we have a negative experience of being fathered as a child, then we have greater difficulty connecting with what father represents in our psyches, usually strength and self-belief.

Bly and others suggest that modern fathers are seen as dejected and weakened. 'We see fathers diminished, reduced to stick-figure cartoons, unable to fare forward or retreat, no match for feisty, furious women'.[1] Consequently, it is hard for the modern father to fit the robes of a king. The diminishment of the father means that there are a great many sons and daughters who harbour a father longing. As women, our need to connect with the king will be activated in particular whenever we fall in love. Seeking to find our inner king we will dress our lover in king's robes and then, when our idealism takes a tumble, we will wonder why they no longer fit him.

As already said, a vast number of children grow up today with no fathers, or 'absent fathers'. It is estimated that over fifty percent of American households function with no father present. The figures may not be that high in Western Europe, but they are increasing. Even when there is a father present, he may not be 'available' to his children because of work or other pressures. Some research suggests that the average amount of time fathers now spend with their children is as little as seven minutes a day. This is causing many problems, both on a psychological and social level.

In childbirth, it is easy to downplay the father's role. After all, he appears to have such an insignificant part to play in the whole process. Added to this is the already mentioned growing phenomenon of single parent families headed by women. These factors reinforce the idea that fathers are dispensable. Kieran McKeown, social researcher and co-author of a book on fathers[2] , points out that traditional roles, where the father works outside the home and the mother in the home, may strengthen the mother's emotional relationship with her children at the expense of the father's. This may unwittingly serve to further devalue the importance of his role in the upbringing of his children.

As already stated, aspects of modern medical fertility treatment also ensures that an absent father culture lives on. Using donor sperm in particular to conceive babies ensures that the father is not only anonymous but also missing. A growing number of babies are born fatherless and the products of disembodied fathers. This has psychological implications. One wonders how the father archetype will be activated in these children. All children need to humanise the mother and father archetypes. A little girl will use her mother as her role model for fleshing out her potential as a woman. Boys will draw on their fathers to give form to their innate masculinity and bring their male souls into the world.

Nature too has arranged it so that father's role is less defined. Unlike the woman who grows the baby inside her and who therefore knows that her child is hers, the father cannot be certain of paternity without a DNA test. Pregnancy and childbirth serve as initiations into the 'blood' mysteries of the feminine. This helps women to be embodied. Men today, in a society increasingly devoid of active initiations, may find it harder to become grounded or embodied. For young girls, menstruation serves as an initiation into womanhood. There is no such 'blood' ritual for boys provided by nature.

Many Jungian psychologists and others have addressed the 'absent father' syndrome both in modern living and in living myth. Myths tell us the basic structures of history and symbolically reveal to us our heritage. The silence of the father and the suffering of the son have been heralded in the Christian myth. According to Guy Corneau, Jungian analyst and author of *Absent Fathers Lost Sons*, the absence and spiritualization of the father have marked our evolution over the past two centuries. A disembodied image of the masculine has been handed down to us though the Judaeo-Christian traditions of discarnate spirituality. Catholic Church teaching has given credence to the notion of the 'caretaker father', namely St Joseph, who though protector of Mary and Jesus, took no active part in the conception.

All these factors influence how we perceive the father. From my own experience of working with couples during childbirth however, I know how important the unborn child's father is in the whole process. Many studies indicate that in pregnancy, mothers who are supported emotionally by their partners generally have better and more fulfilling birth experiences. In today's maternity hospitals, the presence of the child's father in the delivery room has almost become the norm. That practice accepted, men as fathers have not yet found their place in childbirth. Modern medicalised birthing practice tends to marginalise fathers. They are usually spare parts in the midst of hospital machinery and medical staff. Couples who want to avoid making the father feel superfluous opt for home births where the baby's father becomes an integral part of the birth process. In my view this is the ideal scenario.

In writing this book I am adding my voice to those of others for the reinstatement of the 'Fallen King' and lost father. By focusing on the man as son, partner, lover and father, perhaps we will find him in the pages of this book. In the early chapters I will be looking at the role of the father in the bringing to birth of his child. *Father's birth gift* deals very specifically with what the father brings psychologically to his child at birth and in infancy. In *fathers and Sons* I deal with the relationship between fathers and sons and the psychic and mythic images that shape a man. In *Sons and Lovers* I write about men as lovers, partners and fathers. In *Father in the Labour Room* and *Father in the Nursery* I take you into the labour and birth room during birth and examine the early postnatal time. In the final two chapters I write about the need to recover soul by uniting the feminine and masculine energies within us.

A few caveats. Where I write about the experience of babies and small children, I have chosen to refer to the child as 'he' for consistency purposes. And since this book is about reclaiming father and the masculine principle, I have by necessity highlighted the influence of the father on sons rather than daughters. However, the other is implicit since I am also dealing with the father as an inner psychic figure.

Although this book is a personal statement based on many years of experience as a psychotherapist, daughter, lover, wife and mother, I owe a great debt to my clients both male and female who have shared with me the joys and pains of living and loving. I thank all those who have worked with me. All the characters in the book are fictitious in that they are composites, and any clinical material has been disguised so as to protect the identity of those involved. The two dreams quoted towards the end of the book come with the permission of the dreamers.

Through its psychological and spiritual perspective, I hope this book will contribute in its own way to a deepening of understanding of the importance of reclaiming father by recovering the inner king in both men and women.

Notes

1.   R. Bly, *The Hunger for the King in a Time with no Father* in P. Berry, (ed) *Mothers, Fathers* (1991) p12
2.   McKeown, K.; Ferguson H.; Rooney D. *Changing Fathers?* (1998)

CHAPTER ONE

BIRTH
AS SOUL EXPERIENCE

"Before I formed you in the womb, I knew you
Before you came to birth I consecrated you"

(Old Testament Jeremiah cp.1 verse5)

Cifre's life had changed dramatically in the last four months. Not only had she moved home, but she had given up her job, taken up yoga and meditation and was now embarking on a part time course in Buddhist studies. Her husband Andy was finding it hard to believe that this was the woman he had fallen in love with and married. Attracted to her forthright, practical nature, Andy had in the last few years begun to rely on the fact that his wife made a lot of the decisions regarding their life together. He was proud of her ambitious nature and her career as a medical doctor. Now however, he was confused and not a little alarmed. Giving up her job was unsettling enough, but studying Buddhism and spending long hours alone left him feeling concerned. Suddenly, the status quo had changed. From being a two-income family, he was now the sole breadwinner. Although he could cope with that, her sudden interest in spirituality baffled him. Far from seeking to get involved in the practical aspects of their life together, Cifre seemed to be withdrawing. Pre-occupied with an inner world he could not share, Andy wondered if he was losing Cifre. What had happened to his strong practical wife?

Cifre was pregnant. She was happy. Although their baby was planned, Cifre had been unprepared for the tumultuous changes happening inside her. Her body seemed to be taking on a life of it's own and her inner world pulled her into its depths. Pre-occupied and dreamy, she seemed to be listening to an inner conversation that enthralled her. Previously active and self-motivated, she was content to spend hours reading, meditating and singing to her baby. Her dreams blended into her waking life and lately it seemed, voices from the past claimed her attention. Having opened the gate, Cifre wandered into a spiritual landscape that both fascinated and challenged her. Questions opened in her mind and she felt challenged to find answers. Something amazing was happening, and nothing was or would ever be the same again.

The birth of a child is much more than a physical event. It is a deeply spiritual one. For the parents, and most particularly the mother, having a baby is a powerful life changing experience. While the concrete, physical nature of birth is undoubted, it is much less recognised that childbirth is also a spiritual experience. Sometimes it is particularly hard for partners of pregnant women to recognise this aspect of childbirth. Like Andy, husbands and partners of pregnant women are on the outside of the experience. They cannot share the strange and wonderful inner world of pregnancy. They can only observe the changes taking place. Whilst the physical changes are obvious, the psychological changes are not. And so when their partners become dreamy and preoccupied, or suddenly express an interest in things esoteric or spiritual, they are often baffled.

At a pre-and perinatal psychology conference some years ago, I learnt of a beautiful ritual connected to childbirth. A certain East African tribe practises this ritual and it was after hearing it that I finally settled on the name for my book *Songs from the Womb.* When an East African tribal woman decides to have a child, she goes every day and sits quietly under a tree and waits. She waits patiently for a sign from her child to come. Eventually she hears a song. She listens to the song of the child she is about to conceive. When she goes home, she sings this song to her husband and the song is sung again as they make love and the child is conceived. The song is sung when the child is born. It remains the song of that child throughout life and it is sung again, finally, at death. This is a soul song. It is that soul's essence in sound and guides that soul on its human journey.

To me this story encapsulates an aspect of childbirth that

is often neglected. Although it would be easy to regard it as a physical experience only, childbirth is also a soul experience. Hospitals and the medical system generally tend to view childbirth as purely a physical event to be managed by doctors. But every woman who has given birth knows that this is only half the story. Not only does her body change shape so does her soul. A woman who has carried a child, especially if she has listened to her inner self, knows that birth is a soul experience. It is as much a soul experience for the mother giving birth as it is for her child about to come into the world.

SOUL CHANGES IN PREGNANCY

'Before I formed you in the womb, I knew you'.

These words from the Old Testament give us a sense of the spiritual nature of pregnancy and childbirth. When a woman becomes pregnant and carries her child, she enters a whole new world. In addition to the enormous physical and hormonal changes taking place, pregnancy opens a gateway to the spirit world. Her psyche changes, it is more open. Hormonal and psychological influences mean pregnant women are naturally more vulnerable and emotional. A pregnant woman becomes open to the unconscious and to her personal history in a way that is special. Memories of being a child and of being mothered will often surface together with early experiences of family relationships. She will wonder about how other women in her family have coped with pregnancy and childbirth. At night, her long deceased grandmothers and great-grandmothers who come to sing their own particular songs about childbirth may visit her in her dreams. She may have strange thoughts about the baby she is carrying. She may be presented with psychic images from her past and her dreams will be crowded with the lived and the unlived. She is open to all sorts of influences, and her inner world is crowded with images from her unconscious. An expectant mother goes through enormous changes as a result of her pregnancy and the effects of great hormonal shifts in her body. As I said, not only does her body change, so does her soul.

This aspect of childbirth is not often acknowledged. In my last book I addressed the loss of soul that arises as a result of the overly medicalised management of the birth experience. I wrote about the Wounded Mother archetype that the western world has embraced in its denial of choice and autonomy in childbirth. The sometimes violent and invasive birth practices that have become the norm in modern technological childbirth mean that many women and their babies are now emerging from birth rooms traumatised.

Songs from the Womb looks at childbirth from a spiritual and psychological perspective. In doing so, it challenges one of the most pervasive myths of our time, namely that birth is a physical experience to be managed by doctors. It is also about the healing of birth wounds. My objective then, was to highlight what pre-and perinatal psychology tells us, which is that birth and life in the womb is a formative experience. My aim was also to highlight the spiritual and psychological dimensions of pregnancy and childbirth so that changes could be made in the way we birth our babies, and so that increased awareness could inform prenatal and pregnancy care. Based on my work as a therapist and my own personal experience, I know that birth and prenatal life is a conscious soul experience that creates patterns we then carry with us into later life. I know also that there is room for improvement in pregnancy and birth care, and that women and their babies are hurt and affected psychologically by negative birth experiences. Soul wounds inflicted at birth are serious, and we may spend the rest of our lives trying to heal them.

SOUL CHILD

'Before you came to birth I consecrated you'.

Many traditional societies and the Tibetan culture in particular, recognise childbirth as a spiritual experience and this is reflected in the care of pregnant and birthing women. In the West we have tended to view childbirth as purely a physical, biological experience. This is a very one-sided view and one that I believe lies at the root of our medicalised birthing culture. Yet most women who have become pregnant and borne children feel there is more to the experience. Few women emerge from childbirth untouched psychologically or emotionally. There is a spiritual energy to pregnancy and birth. When we want to conceive a child, many of us call our babies to us. Our wish to conceive constellates in us a desire, sometimes a longing. That desire has its own energy and sends out a signal that attracts energy back. Long before there is a child the child exists in the thoughts of the mother and sometimes the father. As children, eager to know of our beginnings we are often told 'you were only a gleam in your father's eye'! Sometimes however, pregnancy comes to us unplanned and may take us by surprise. Then it is our babies' unborn souls that call to us from some place between the earth and the sky when they decide to incarnate through us. Let me explain this.

Writing from both a Jungian and a spiritual perspective, I believe the soul's journey does not end in one lifetime. Life is a continuum, and our soul's existence may span many embodiments. We choose our embodiments in line with our spiritual challenges. This means that a soul wishing to incarnate will seek out the particular parents and circumstances that will offer it the greatest opportunities for growth. Once born the new soul has incarnated and must begin its chosen journey in the world. A newborn has not long left the spirit world and it still carries the Divine as a recent memory. Babies come straight from God. You can see soul in a newborn baby's eyes. Everything I have ever learnt about soul has been through my work with babies both born and unborn.

I heard a story once which moved me greatly and which I recount frequently to the groups I work with. A little girl awaited with great eagerness the birth of her sibling. Her mother went into hospital to have the baby and at last the great day came when her little baby brother was brought home. The little girl, eager to be alone with her new brother kept insisting her parents leave them in a room together. Her parents, concerned about the possibility that sibling rivalry might get out of hand, reluctantly agreed but not before they had hooked up the baby intercom so they could hear what was going on in case of a problem. The little girl thanked them and gravely shut the door. She approached her little brother's cradle and bending low, she said 'little baby, remind me what God looks like, I'm beginning to forget'.

The medicalisation of childbirth may have brought many benefits but it has been at a spiritual cost. As a society we all suffer the cost. As a mother, therapist and prenatal teacher working in London, England in the 1980s, I became very aware of how mothers and babies were disempowered by the birth experience when it 'went wrong'. This was usually in hospitals where the labour was medically managed. Women were emerging from modern birth rooms, where technology had replaced nature, very badly hurt and even damaged. Their babies were hurt too. This is because if the birth experience is a shattering or traumatic one for the mother, then it will also be so for her baby. Mother and baby are so linked together at this time that there can be no psychological and maybe even physical damage to one without the other being affected. However, the wounds I refer to here are soul wounds.

In the 1980s I founded and ran a Holistic Birth Centre where pregnant women and couples came to prepare for the birth of their babies. Very often, despite great awareness and preparation, I saw mothers return after the birth, hurt and disillusioned. Many felt demeaned and disempowered by a medical system that appeared largely ignorant of their soul needs and those of their babies. Often a mother was not allowed to follow the dictates of her body and so had to endure a technological birth very different from what she had imagined. The medical establishment's fear and suspicion of nature meant that violent and invasive birth practices were common. Unfortunately, they still are.

Birth is an experience that is deeply engraved on our souls. It leaves traces that permeate our lives. My training in Jungian depth psychology, along with my studies in pre-and perinatal psychology, my clinical work and my own growing spiritual awareness have helped me come to this conclusion. Jungian psychology, based on the work of Swiss psychiatrist and psychologist CGJung, establishes giving birth and being born as archetypal experiences of profound emotional and spiritual significance. Pre-and perinatal psychology, which is the study of prenatal and perinatal life and its importance in later life, demonstrates clearly that birth and life in the womb are formative experiences creating patterns that we carry with us into future life. Additionally, for the mother, pregnancy and childbirth represent a time of transformation, an initiatory experience. A woman changes forever when she becomes a mother. She creates life, transforming essence into matter like an alchemist. Symbolically speaking, she is transformed in the process of giving birth to her child.

AN INITIATION

CGJung talked about archetypes as primordial images that inform our psyches, our souls. An archetypal experience is a primal experience, universal in nature and origin. Birth and death are such experiences. If a woman has a bad or difficult birthing experience, it permeates her soul, and her transition to motherhood is thus marked. Similarly, for the child about to be born, coming into the world is a unique initiation. The manner in which a child comes into the world will affect all future initiations in the life of that child. First day at school, leaving home, getting married, becoming a parent. All these are initiations. Initiations involve a kind of test, a letting go of the past and moving forward to the next phase of life. Birth is our first initiation. It is a struggle, a struggle that all of nature mirrors. Compare the physical experience of birth with that of a flower. The poet Dylan Thomas writes,

'The force that through the green fuse drives the
flower Drives my green age.'

Even a flower has to push up through the earth in order to come to life, sprouting from the earth that created and nurtured it. Dylan Thomas continues,

'The force that drives the water through the rocks
Drives my red blood'

The physical experience of birth in this sense is a necessary struggle, an initiation into life outside the womb. It follows that the way in which that initiation happens is of major importance to the child coming into being. The experience is formative in nature. A newborn will carry into the world both its prenatal experience and that of its passage into life, its birth. Prenatal and birth memory exists in all of us, hidden in the deepest recesses of our psyches and the finest fibres of our cells.

In my last book I wrote about the different types of initiations, births by caesarean section for example. A baby born by caesarean will have a very different experience than that of a child born normally, i.e. vaginally. It will not have the same internal sense of a successful struggle to come to birth. Psychologically speaking, natural birth is an ego-enhancing experience. Birth is a struggle that the baby must overcome in order to survive. At a fundamental psychological level, the baby's ability to survive the intensity and strain of the birth experience means a successful initiation, which teaches it about its ability to struggle and survive in the face of life's difficulties. For example, if the birth is normal and the baby is born by its own and its mother's efforts, an internalised feeling of success in the face of struggle may result. It may also mean that emotional and psychological separation from the mother later on in life will be facilitated in some way. If the child is born normally, then a natural physical separation has occurred. But if a child has to be torn or extracted from its mother, then emotional separation is made more difficult, because it is as if the birth had taken place reluctantly.

In a normal birth, the model established is of natural separation in its own time. A child born by caesarean section, particularly non- labour caesarean is, however, deprived of its birth struggle. The infant is suddenly removed from its mother and has no time to prepare for life outside the womb. One minute it is in the womb, the next it is out in the world. Non-labour caesarean babies, unlike their labour counterparts, have no sense of struggle, or of a birth process. They are simply 'pulled out' suddenly. They are denied the struggle to be born. This does not of course mean that they have not had their own particular struggle in the womb. But, if we are to consider birth as the unique initiation that it undoubtedly is, theirs is different. Whichever way the birth happens, it is formative. Psychological research studies indicate that the experience remains with the child, re-emerging usually when triggered by a future traumatic life experience.

LIFE IN THE WOMB

Even before birth the child has experiences. When he emerges from the womb he already has a history and a story to tell. He will have experienced good and bad, love and pain and a great many other emotions. As I said earlier, pre and perinatal psychology and observational studies confirm without a doubt that both life in the womb and the birth experience are formative. Not long ago however, it was thought that life in the womb didn't count in psychological terms. It didn't count because it was believed that mental life began at or after birth. Unborn babies did not have the ability to feel or to think. The traditional medical view was that since the cerebral cortex of the newborn, not to mention the unborn child, is not fully myelinated, there can be no memory of either life in the womb or the birth experience itself. However, ample and increasing research not only in medicine but also in the field of consciousness research, experiential psychotherapy and pre and perinatal psychology show beyond a doubt that the unborn baby is very aware of, and affected by his environment. Recent observational studies tells us that the unborn baby is not merely a developing biological organism but a sophisticated evolving human being of immense sensitivity and capability. The child in the womb has been shown to be capable of learning, memorising, dreaming and even socialising!

There are many books now available about the nature of life in the womb. Perhaps the most notable is *The Secret Life of the Unborn Child*.[1] My own book *Songs from the Womb* also contains many references and case examples. Recent work by the Italian psychoanalyst Allesandra Piontelli, whose observational study of the behaviour of unborn babies by ultrasound scanning is described in her book *From Fetus to Child*[2], indicates that there is continuity of behaviour between prenatal and post-natal life. Other studies have found that unborn babies have innate personalities as well as likes and dislikes, and there is continuity of behaviour in post-natal life. The sum of this work indicates that unborn babies are 'conscious' and profoundly affected by their womb life experience.

Mothers know this instinctively. But because of an endemic and pervasive cultural climate that makes us doubt what we know or makes us forget what we know, the wisdom of this instinctive knowledge is then lost. In a culture which honours thinking and doing rather than being and intuition, it's easy to lose your way. It is easy to feel disconnected from our inner wisdom. And we feel soul loss as a result. We feel soul loss every time we deny our inner truth. This happens frequently in childbirth when a birthing mother's inner voice is challenged or ignored. How often do we hear stories of mothers in labour telling the birth attendants their baby is about to be born, only to be told 'no you can't possibly be ready yet'. The child is often born very soon afterwards, much to the surprise and disarmament of birth attendants who are not ready to receive the baby.

A WOMB WITH A VIEW

Interest in the psychological effects of the birth experience has been around for a long time. We are all familiar with the concept of birth trauma. However, the idea not only that prenatal life is significant to future life and development, but also that mother's thoughts and feelings affect her unborn baby, is relatively new. Unborn babies do indeed have a 'secret life'. We know that they react to changes in their womb environment. Such changes may be induced in the womb as a result of the mother's emotional state or as a result of substances ingested directly by her. Unborn babies also have reactions to intrusive medical procedures and chemicals introduced into the womb. American psychologist, researcher and author David Chamberlain published many of his findings in his book *Babies Remember Birth*[3]. His research indicates that unborn babies are acutely sensitive to events in the womb and to their mother's thoughts and feelings. His research also indicates that neonates are reportedly very well tuned to their mother's emotional state and find it very painful to be taken away from their mothers at birth.

Chamberlain's work confirms the interrelationship of mother and child. They are inextricably linked in the way described by English Paediatrician DW Winnicott who stated that there are no babies, only mothers and babies. What affects mother affects her baby. For nine long months as the baby grows inside his mother he grows used to her frequency. He learns her heart song, he learns her rhythm, and he responds accordingly. By the time that he is born, a child will know his mother in a way that he will know no one else. He has resonated to her vibration, her frequency. He tunes in to her, he has to do that in order to survive.

An unborn baby responds to its mother's moods, feelings and thoughts as well as to her physical space. A baby feels and experiences the womb with its histories and its energies. Most babies will seek a womb with a view and often receive a dusty answer, for they will inhabit a womb space that will have its own particular brand of nuances and echoes from the past. Perhaps this womb has already housed a sibling and her song still resonates inside its walls. Perhaps this womb has suffered previous death, and so sadness permeates its cells. *In Songs from the Womb* I wrote about a baby who grew inside her mother in an atmosphere of fear created by previous deaths. This early conditioning stayed with her so that as an adult she was 'drawn towards death'.[4]

Prenates incorporate parental experiences and feelings. This means that unborn babies absorb parental expectations, and just as children are destined to live out their parents' unlived lives, babies in the womb are marked by their parents' thoughts and feelings. This makes sense. Spirit permeates matter to create new life, and the womb is a place where psyche is given form. This form we take with us out into the world. Soul transcends biography but is marked by it. Although we may find it hard to accept that something as intangible as a thought or a feeling may have an effect, this is so. We know that our thoughts can affect and even create our reality. Psyche and soma, body and soul are connected. If for example, a mother wants her unborn baby to be a boy and wishes this all though her pregnancy and has expectations about what this boy will become, her unborn baby will be aware of this. If her baby is in fact a girl, she may be amused or confused by this expectation. She will be affected, albeit unconsciously so.

Sheila was once such girl. She first came to see me because she had some difficulty with her sexual orientation. In the course of our work together we uncovered, through birth regression, that her parents had conceived her with the thought, 'let's try for a boy'. Parents of three girls, they really wanted their fourth child to be a boy. Sheila's confusion regarding her sexual identity has originated in the womb. She was a woman, but she should have been a boy!

FINELY TUNED

Unborn babies are very finely tuned to their mothers and react accordingly. Babies move in response to mother's cough or laugh. Between 10 and 15 weeks, mother's laugh or cough will get most fetuses moving within seconds[5]. I remember this in my own case. When six months pregnant with my eldest son, I went into a fit of the giggles and ended up exhausted, tears streaming down my face. My son started dancing around in my womb in a way that he had not done previously or indeed for such an extended period. I could only imagine he wanted to join in the fun!

There are more dramatic examples. Babies have been observed by ultrasound reacting to the amniocentesis needle being inserted into the womb during medical tests. Understandably threatened, one 16-week fetus caught the barrel of the needle in his hand much to the amazed distress of the anaesthetist. Many babies move around during ultrasound scanning also. My daughter at 22 weeks kept moving away out of sight of the scanner, as though she did not wish to be seen.

Chamberlain makes the point that 'babies do not live in a fortress but in a mother'[6]. If she is assaulted, babies will learn about violence; if she is loved, babies will learn about love. If a mother is hurt, either physically or emotionally during her pregnancy, the child will be aware of this. A fetus whose mother received an electric shock while she was doing some ironing sat bolt upright and immobile in the womb for two days, long after the mother had recovered. Researcher Inez Correia[7] has measured the effect on the fetus of a mother viewing brief clips of a violent movie. The fetus became upset along with the mother.

The unborn baby's spontaneous movements (as opposed to reflexes) have also been observed through ultrasound. These movements represent chosen activities by the babies, such as daily exercising, swimming around in the amniotic fluid, sucking their thumbs and scratching their heads. At eight weeks, the fetus already enjoys a surprising degree of mobility, range of movement and activity, and as early as the seventh week Central Nervous System (CNS) reflexes can be shown. It appears that each baby has its own exercise routine. Some choose to move around much more than others. At little more than 16 weeks Rapid Eye Movement (REM) sleep is observed. This indicates that unborn babies enjoy a dream life from very early on. Extensive research shows that all human senses are operative by at least early in the second trimester (three to six months). The unborn baby may not be ready for life outside the womb, but it is already very mature in many senses of the word.

I CAN HEAR: I CAN SOCIALISE

Very few people will be surprised to learn that unborn babies can hear. However recent studies indicate that not only can the fetus hear but also it is capable of learning and memorising sound as the following French study demonstrates. Every evening women were asked to read out loud to their unborn babies of between 32 and 37 weeks, a fairy story of their choice. After birth, the babies not only demonstrated recognition of the story that had been read to them in the womb, they also reacted in utero with a consistent lowering of the heartbeat as the story was read to them[7].

Unborn babies respond to different types of music and are said to react well to Mozart, Brahms and Vivaldi but badly to Beethoven, Wagner and also loud rock music, as one pregnant woman discovered! She had attended a rock concert late in her pregnancy, but had to leave half way through because her unborn baby began to kick vigorously and continued to agitate in protest to the music. The fact that an unborn baby can hear is also demonstrated by the way a newborn recognises not only its mother's voice but also that of its father. This is particularly noticeable in instances where the father of the child has been talking to it before birth.

Observational studies also show that babies interact socially from very early on. For example, Piontelli's study on twins in utero shows quite clearly that as early as 16 weeks the fetus is capable of interactive social behaviour. During regular ultrasound scanning, one twin (a boy) was observed to be consistently more active in the uterine environment than his sister who generally slept peacefully, curled up in her corner of the womb. Under ultrasound observation the following behaviour patterns by the twins was noted. Every so often, the more active boy would approach his sister, stroking the membrane between them, encouraging her to play. She would wake up and the twins would play together in their mother's womb, moving around behind their respective membranes. Piontelli continued to observe these babies' behaviour after their birth. She found that as toddlers their favourite game was to play with a curtain between them! They would box and tickle one another, stroking and poking the curtain that divided them. Boxing matches have also been observed between brothers in the womb! All of this shows that by age 20 weeks, many twins manifest with different types of behaviour ranging from affectionate to aggressive.

Another example from Piontelli tells a very interesting story of how womb life experience affected a little girl. Pina's story demonstrates very clearly the continuity of behaviour from prenatal to postnatal life. Also, and more importantly in this case, it is the formative quality of the prenatal experience and the way in which it remains a memory that inevitably colours post womb life. Piontelli observed Pina through ultrasound scan at four week intervals from 16 weeks of gestational age to birth and thereafter to three years of age. At the first two observations Pina could be seen to be actively exploring her uterine environment. She moved a lot and was seen to be extremely active in the womb. Shortly after the second ultrasound observation in which Pina was seen to play with and pull on the placenta, Pina's mother suffered a near miscarriage due to a partial detachment of the placenta. She was ordered complete rest and the miscarriage was averted. The effect on Pina was dramatic however. When next observed, she was curled up tightly in the corner of the womb, immobile. She remained so for virtually the entire remainder of the pregnancy and, at delivery, (which was by Caesarean section) she was found to be deeply lodged in the womb and difficult to 'get out'.

In postnatal observations, Pina's behaviour indicated a pattern of active, almost manic exploration of her environment, followed by periods of great anxiety. These were often of a claustrophobic nature and rendered her immobile and fearful. Her mother was reported as saying that Pina was especially terrified of water and hated being washed. She would cling to the side of her baby bath and scream as her mother tried to wash her: 'It was as if she were afraid of being washed away'. The experience of the near miscarriage seems to have affected Pina in such a way that she carried it with her as an unconscious memory, and it undoubtedly coloured and influenced her postnatal behaviour.

The fact that this observational study shows the existence of characteristic behaviour by each fetus, and the fact that this behaviour also continues in later life, indicates the existence of innate predispositions. What is also important to note, is that Piontelli's observational study shows clearly how womb events such as threatened miscarriage severely affect the fetus and are responsible for reactive behaviour well into postnatal life. Again this indicates something which may seem perfectly obvious to mothers as well as prenatal psychologists i.e. that babies have a memory and that events in the womb are recorded somewhere in the unconscious mind.

I CAN FEEL LOVE AND PAIN

As referred to earlier it is apparent that unborn babies are capable of affectionate behaviour and a range of feelings. Studies on adults who suffered the loss of a twin while in the womb indicate that the experience was a traumatic one, with the surviving twin sustaining a great sense of loss and grief. This loss, especially if unmourned, can present as depression in later life. The experience of loss can leave its mark on the unborn child. It can span years and even generations. I recall one case of a little boy who suffered from profound cyclical depressions and whose mother took him to see a psychologist. She herself had suffered the loss of her father while pregnant with him. She had been profoundly upset during her pregnancy. When he was depressed and withdrawn, the little boy would draw pictures of old men dying in caves, a profound image of what he had internalised in the womb, the walls of which resounded with the loss of his grandfather. It appears that this mother's grief had affected her unborn baby. The womb he inhabited was a sad place for him.

Stories like this are not uncommon. It is impossible to avoid feeling pain or grief while pregnant, because it is part of life. However, awareness that thoughts, feelings and emotions are transmitted to the baby in the womb enables us to heal, or to begin to heal. If we accept that life in the womb is a place where we learn about the joys and pains of human life, then we can help transform negative or painful patterns that originate there.

Very small babies are capable of loving and bonding. Babies are loving by nature. I believe that since babies are much closer to the Divine that we are, they are capable of unconditional love in a way that adults are not. As we grow older and more used to our human journey, we have a tendency to forget our spiritual natures. We forget that we are

really souls clothed in a human body and we have more difficulty reconnecting with our capacity to love. Babies too, particularly if they have very negative experiences in the womb
and at birth, will also begin to forget. If a baby's love is not
accepted and responded to, it suffers soul loss. The experience of soul loss is very painful, for it is in our natures to be
whole and to seek wholeness. It is also in our natures to bond
with our mothers and other care givers, and every baby is
primed to do so.

Regression therapy demonstrates that babies find separation from their mothers at birth very painful, particularly if
this separation happens before time, as in a premature birth.
This is why it is recognised to be so important for the newborn
to be handed to its mother as soon as possible after birth. Skin
to skin contact is a vital part of the bonding process, and
babies who are separated from their mothers at birth are
always at risk of impaired bonding. If there is any lack of harmony in the birth process it affects mother and baby bonding.
All babies expect to be welcomed at birth and to be with their
mothers. Again it is a basic archetypal instinct. It is an innate
expectation.

Most premature babies will have to spend some time in
an incubator, deprived of the warmth of human skin contact
except for brief periods when they are changed and some of
their physical needs attended to. The very tiny ones may be
fed by tubes so that even the act of feeding does not necessarily mean human contact. With who or what do they bond?
Since we know that they and their siblings still in the womb
are capable of affectionate behaviour, we must ask ourselves
what these little human beings are learning about life, and
what they are suffering.

Those who have worked with premature babies have
observed that they respond extremely well to human contact,
and obviously feel deprived without it. The midwife who tours
the special care baby unit every night, checking each tiny
inmate, knows this, as she sees how those who are strong
enough wedge themselves against the wall of their incubator,
as if seeking contact with something or someone. Experiments
and studies by Doctors Ray and Martinez in Chile showed that
premature babies thrive when, instead of being confined all
the time to incubators, they are carried around kangaroo fash-
ion between the breasts of midwives. Others have noted the

importance of a loving environment to premature babies and strive to create such an environment in special care units. Even having hospital staff sit and talk about a baby whilst sitting around his or her incubator has been shown to have a beneficial effect. Babies who are thought about and loved thrive. Those who are emotionally neglected do less well.

PRENATAL LEARNING

The womb is a child's first school. Unborn babies learn in the womb. Researchers at Queens University Belfast, in Ireland have contributed much of the evidence that the unborn baby is capable of learning. The research team at the Fetal Research Centre concentrate on the adaptive functions of prenatal learning for life after birth and discuss evidence for prenatal learning in the fetus. Studies demonstrate that the fetus familiarises itself with the diet of the mother while still in the womb through the amniotic fluid, and this influences its sucking behaviour after birth. This is because the amniotic fluid and mother's breast milk smell the same. The baby in the womb of course, regularly swallows the amniotic fluid. It explains why babies whose mothers have changed their diets before and immediately after birth have much more difficulty establishing breast-feeding than those babies whose mothers' diets remain unchanged. Studies of Asian women, who have their babies in Northern Ireland and whose diet changed dramatically for a few days while in hospital, indicate that they had greater difficulty in establishing breastfeeding. This it considered to be due to the altered taste and smell of the breast milk caused by the change in diet.

It is suggested therefore that the ability of the fetus to learn whilst still in the womb has evolved as an essential tool for its life after birth. It also ensures that when the time comes for it to be born the baby is equipped to survive in its new environment. Many other studies are also emerging which demonstrate the ability of the unborn baby to learn and respond to external conditioning. This knowledge has encouraged prospective parents to communicate with their unborn babies through massage, touch, sound and even thought. Mothers know that even thinking in a positive loving way about their babies produces a sense of harmony that the child feels and enjoys.

BIRTH AND VIOLENCE

Despite our growing awareness of the 'secret life of the unborn child' and the formative nature of the birth experience, we don't have to search too far for confirmation that all is not well in the birth rooms of the world. One cannot help but wonder if there is a human cost associated with modern birth practice where technology has, by and large, replaced nature. It seems sad to have to place the words birth and violence side by side. What is even more alarming is the fact that the two can be linked and that evidence suggests that our modern approach to childbirth has brought about this situation.

Research based on more than 4,600 consecutive births in Copenhagen found that birth complications such as the use of forceps, breech delivery, cord prolapse, pre-eclampsia and long labour, when combined with maternal rejection and extended separations in the first year, predispose the victims towards violent crime.[9] Earlier studies found links between obstetric complications and behaviour disorders in children[10], perinatal trauma and juvenile delinquency,[11] and perinatal complications and criminality[12].

Psychologists who reviewed the effects of maternal anaesthetics on infants showed lasting effects on both their behaviour and their muscular function. Many children born to mothers who were given drugs during labour were slow to start sitting, standing and walking. By the age of seven some of these children were lagging in language learning skills, perception, memory and judgement. In Sweden, Jacobson and colleagues studied the birth experience of adult addicts and found a connection between obstetric pain medication and eventual amphetamine addiction[12].

The link between drugs, alcohol, difficult births and the incidence of learning disabilities and emotional disorders is well recognised by educators and particularly by those who work with disabled and special needs children. Prenatal and birth trauma impair bonding at birth. Lack of bonding in particular predisposes the individual to aggression and violence and difficulties with relating. And so the cycle goes on.

As a society we are no strangers to violence or to social and psychological unrest. Neither are we strangers to soul pain. However, it is only relatively recently that psychological boundaries have shifted enough to accept that the prenatal and birth experience are important influences on later life. It is through this awareness that the source of very painful and destructive behaviour can be traced. As I said earlier, some psychologists believe that the roots of violence are being sown every day in the birth rooms of the world. As a psychotherapist and birth teacher, what I see is that soul wounds are inflicted every time a baby is born without due regard for the manner in which it is born. And a soul wound is created every time a mother feels psychological pain relating to her birth experience and it is not acknowledged as such. As a therapist in clinical practice, I am often brought into the womb life and the birth experience of my clients. It is here that particular patterns of relating and behaviour originate. It is here that a soul wound can lie. Increasing evidence suggests that everything that happens in the womb is recorded somewhere in the child's unconscious. Echoes of prenatal life experience often enter the therapy or consulting room. I hear and sense these echoes in the men and women who come to see me. I feel their presence in the relationships and attachment patterns that my clients unravel before me. I see them emerge in dreams and other unconscious processes.

SOUL SONG

To go back to the soul song; all children want their parents to listen to their song. They want to be responded to. They will sing their song for so long and if they receive no reply, they will gradually cease to sing. They will shut down. During the course of a congress some years ago, I watched a video of newborn babies filmed in an Eastern European hospital nursery. The newborns were filmed over a period of 24 hours after birth. All reacted differently to being separated from their mothers, but all cried for longer or shorter periods of time before eventually crying themselves to sleep. I recall one particularly lusty baby who cried loudly and consistently for an extended period of time and then fell into an exhausted sleep. When she woke she again began to cry. Gradually over time, her cries became quieter and shorter until they died down altogether. It was poignant to watch. It was as if by not receiving any response she had given up. A part of her began to shut down.

FATHERS AND BIRTH

Accepting that birth is a soul experience means being mindful that the soul of the child incarnating is already very aware. The child will not only seek out a mother but it will also seek out a father. These images are archetypally imprinted in the psyche of the child, therefore father's role in the whole process of the child's coming into being is extremely important. Parents humanise the archetype of the masculine and the feminine for their children. This means that a child's parents *make real* that child's idea of what male and female is, as well as their expectation of being parented. A child's healthy psychological development involves identification with parental figures.

A girl child needs to identify with her mother to gain access to her femininity, to clothe her bones and draw her female soul into the world. A boy child needs his father in order to fully incarnate as a man. If his father is absent, then the boy will use as a reference point other male figures, and he will draw on the dim memories of his grandfather and great-grandfather to give flesh to his indigenous maleness. He will also draw as a matter of course on his mother's animus or male side.

The same happens with girls. If a little girl loses her mother early in her life she will draw on other female figures as mother substitutes. She will also be influenced by her father's inner feminine, but she will have a mother hunger. This mother hunger will drive many of her actions and unconsciously influence her life in many ways. The more remote or absent the child's connection with his parents, the more the child will be influenced by the archetypal mother and father and the more difficult it will be for him to incarnate his own soul. A child needs guidance. An incoming soul needs and seeks out parents to guide it on its journey. Without these flesh and blood human figures as role models, a child will have to rely on remoter parental substitutes and internal parental imagery.

The father's role and influence are very different to those of the mother. I will deal with this in more detail in the next and following chapters. What is important here is to acknowledge the father's contribution to childbirth principally as the supporter and the guardian of his partner. Traditionally, the father has always played a caretaker guardian role for his partner during pregnancy and labour. During the nine months of pregnancy the father's role was to both provide for, and to nurture and support the expectant mother. In most cultures, the strong and committed presence of the father was important on an emotional level as it was clear that pregnant women who felt loved carried their babies happily and gave birth more easily. Childbirth however was actually the province of women, though the father was not necessarily excluded. Leaving the work of childbirth to women, usually it was the female relatives of the woman in labour who acted as midwives, the father instead kept guard and ensured that the women were left undisturbed.

This is by and large no longer the case. In modern birth rooms, where birth has largely become the province of the medical attendants, the father's role and presence have taken on a different character. Up until the early 1970s, fathers were rarely present in the room when their child was born. Most fathers sat nervously in hospital waiting rooms and were called when their child had been born. Still others sat with friends in the local pub, waiting. More recently however, with the advent of more active birth practices, it has almost become the norm for fathers to be present at the birth. This is usually at the request of the mother and it is seen as a good thing. The presence of a supportive partner has been found to shorten labour and helps the woman giving birth. When giving birth in an alien and unnatural environment such as a hospital, women in labour need this emotional support so that they can relax into the process of giving birth.

Most modern women expect to have their partners present at the birth of their children. However, there are a growing number of women who prefer to labour with other women present. Much also depends on whether the birth takes place at home or in hospital. In my role as 'birth teacher' I have attended many births, the majority of which involved working with couples rather than individuals. So, I have had the chance to observe fathers during the birth of their children. My own view is that sometimes it is good for the father to be present in the labour room, sometimes not. It largely depends on the particular relationship the parents have with each other. If it is a good and harmonious relationship, then having the father in attendance will enhance the process. Conversely, if there are any underlying tensions in the relationship then it may surface during labour and operate as a block to the flow of labour.

I have often observed and 'felt' this block. In a particular case, I recall that it was only when I left the room with the husband of a woman who had been in labour for quite some considerable time that she relaxed. Her energy freed up so much that when we returned half an hour later she had dilated four centimetres! He had been tense and irritable and quite understandably exhausted after 24 sleepless hours. But it was his unconscious fears and his resistance to his wife's desire to avoid medication and have a 'natural' birth that were actually blocking the process! In the porous energy and atmosphere of labour she had felt this, and her body had responded by 'clamming up'. However, the opposite can also be true. I have seen and felt a labouring woman open and relax to the almost palpable love and support of her husband. His presence during the birth of his child enhanced the experience for all concerned, but especially for the mother and the emerging child.

In a home birth the father may be present as a matter of course. He may assume responsibility for attending to other children in the family if there are any. He may not be able to help his wife physically give birth, but he can 'be there' for her. If he has a well-developed *Anima* or female side then this will make him a good birth partner because he will pick up on the sensitivities of the process. However, most men are 'doers' by nature and so for many of them it is hard to resist intervening in some way. Some cannot help themselves and so end up trying to 'coach' their partners. 'Remember the classes, do it this way' and so on. Of course this tends to aggravate the situation as labour is not a process that can or should be controlled. Basic instinctual processes have their own natural rhythm and pace. Giving birth calls on some ancient part of us, older than time. Imposing a structure or routine on such an archetypal event tends to disrupt the natural order and create disharmony. The partner who is likely to help the labouring woman most is the one who simply is fully present. To 'be there' pure and simply without having to 'do' anything is all that is needed. In a way it is something akin to the process of therapy. Being there without expectations or desires for a particular outcome facilitates and allows a process to happen.

The presence of fathers in modern birth rooms is an attempt to re-establish childbirth as belonging to the parents. In this sense it is a very positive evolvement. It means that fathers have the opportunity to be there at the very moment their child comes into the world. In many cases this helps the father bond with his child. It enhances the experience of fatherhood. For women, having their partner present means that in most cases they have the emotional security they need to feel safe to give birth. In general it has a positive influence on the way birth is managed in hospitals. Parental control and greater autonomy for the birthing mother have evolved as a result of the greater involvement of both parents in childbirth.

Notes

1. T. Verny, *The Secret Life of the Unborn Child* Sphere Books, (1982)
2. A. Piontelli , *From Fetus to Child* Routledge, (1992)
3. D. Chamberlain, *Babies Remember Birth* Ballantine Books, (1988)
4. B. Mauger, *Songs From the Womb* Collins Press, (1998),p.156
5. A., Ianniruberto, & E Tajani,. *Seminars in Perinatology*, 5 (2) 1981
6. Chamberlain, in *Pre-and Perinatal Psychology Jrn.* 10 (2) 1995
7. I. Correia, Quoted in above
8. A. De Casper,.& W.Fifer,. in *Infant Behaviour & Development* 17(2) 1994 pp159-164
9. A Raine,. et al. *Archives of General Psychiatry* 51 (1994) pp984-988
10. B. Pasamanick, *American Jrn. Psychiatry* 112 (1956) pp613-617
11. D. Lewis, et al *American Jrn Psychiatry* 145 (1979) pp584-589
12. S. Litt, Perinatal *Complications and Criminality*. Doctoral Dissertation, Univ. Michigan, USA
13. B. Jacobson, et al. in *British Medical Jrn.* 301 (1988) pp1067-1070

PART ONE

FATHERS AND BIRTH

CHAPTER TWO

FATHER IN THE LABOUR ROOM

It was bad enough. But to her it was never deathly. Even the fierce, tearing pain was exhilarating. She screamed and suffered, but was all the time alive and vital. She felt so powerfully alive and in the hands of such a masterly force of life, that her bottom-most feeling was one of exhilaration. She knew she was winning, winning, she was always winning, with each onset of pain she was nearer to victory.

(DH Lawrence, The Rainbow)

The power of birth is truly awesome. When you are involved in it you are enveloped by its energy and if you do not resist, you are totally pulled into the experience. If you are the one giving birth then you have no choice but to go with the powerful urges of your body. Birth is an intensely physical event. It is also a spiritual event. It is the birthing of spirit through the body. To observe and to assist a woman give birth is to stand in awe of the beauty and power of nature and our Divine selves. In the great majority of cases birth takes place without any outside intervention. It is a natural, instinctual process as old as time.

What is the experience like for the father of the child, who watches as his child come into the world? I have spoken with many men and I have listened to their stories of birth, of what it felt like to be part of such an event. Most were enthralled by the process, some were distressed but all were touched at being present when their child came into the world. In my last book, I focussed on the birth experience from the mother's perspective. Father was seen as a supporter of the process. Here I will concentrate on birth from the father's perspective.

HOME BIRTH

The father most certainly does have a place in childbirth. He has a very real place, but it is one that as yet hasn't been clearly defined. In home births, he is much more involved in the birth and he has a chance to feel that he has a purposeful if not vital role. As I referred to earlier, men have a function as guardians and protectors of their partners who are giving birth. A man can never enter fully into the birth experience. At best he can only imagine how it feels. He must always remain on the outside as an observer of the power of birth. Nevertheless he can facilitate the process by being present at the event and supporting his partner.

In a home birth situation he may have the task of looking after other children in the house. If the couple are using a birthing pool for example, he may be busy filling it and making sure the water is the right temperature and so on. He will make sure the room is the way his partner wants it to be so that she can feel free to give birth. Or he may be busy dealing with practical matters such as making sure that the woman giving birth is protected from the intrusions of normal day to day activities. If she is worried about another child in the house for example, she will not be able to let go fully. Alternatively, she may feel she needs to protect her partner or other people from the birth process and any expressions of pain she makes during labour. Birthing women are extremely sensitive to the environment and to possible intrusions. She needs to feel very safe to go with the dictates of nature and her own body. Many women need privacy to give birth, something that is much more easily achieved at home than in a hospital.

Privacy and the need to feel safe are, I believe, one of the birthing woman's most fundamental requirements. I remember when I was giving birth to my daughter at home, my sister had to deal with my son's little friend who had quite innocently come in to the house to ask if he could come out to play! I remember being grateful for her presence and for the presence of my husband whom I felt was protecting the house. Throughout, I was keenly aware of the need for privacy and at one point, while I was in the middle of strong labour I went out into the garden to a quiet and private spot, much to the concern of my midwife! I needed to be alone at that point.

By saying a father can also have a role as protector of the birthing space for his partner, I mean that his presence will be valuable to her emotionally so that she can feel free to flow with the birthing energy. This will be particularly the case if she does not have any women friends or relatives in attendance at the birth. Father's presence enhances the mother's birth experience if he has the ability to be emotionally containing. If he feels confident, secure and grounded, then his presence will help the birthing woman. He will be able to calm her down and soothe her when she feels anxious or when the pain becomes difficult for her to cope with. He will be tuned in to her energy so that he knows when to intervene and when to do nothing. If he is so tuned, instinctively, he will know when to speak and when to stay quiet, when to hold her and when to remain at a distance. The energy of birth is very powerful, but it can also be very unpredictable. Sometimes, the woman in labour may need to be alone to deal with the intensity of what she is feeling. Sometimes she may want her partner there all the time. Labour moves and increases in intensity. Like the waves of the sea which are powerless against the movement of the wind, if she is to follow the dictates of her body, the labouring woman will be totally focussed on what is happening inside her. She has no choice.

A woman in labour will have no time for trivial questions or idle chitchat. If he is in tune with her, her partner will know this intuitively. The language of birth is that of the body. The only sounds will be those of the woman in labour and perhaps music if the couple have opted to have it playing in the background. Women need to feel free to cry out and make whatever sounds come naturally from them during labour and the birth itself. Some prenatal teachers encourage women to sing or chant during labour, the theory being that opening the throat and chest allows a free flow of energy and breath. This is necessary to avoid tensing up or holding on. I have always encouraged my clients to do this because deep breathing from the belly, the centre of the body allows the body to move with the forces of birth.

Ideally the father will be alert to any possible interruptions or intrusions from outside which may disturb his partner. If there are other people present, he may ask them to be quiet if he senses they are bothering her. Since having a baby at home is still the prerogative of relatively few couples, those who choose this option will be very connected to the spiritual nature of birth and to the new baby's need for a gentle and respectful transition into life. Both parents are likely to be aware that birth is a soul experience and they will want to be active participants in what should be a joyous and fulfilling experience free from unnecessary medical intervention. It is often parents who have previously gone through a medicalised hospital birth and who were unhappy about it, who subsequently choose a home birth. They do this because they want to feel actively involved and part of the process in a way that is not possible to achieve in a hospital setting.

FATHER AS SUPPORTER AND GUARDIAN

I believe it should not be mandatory for fathers to be present at the birth of their babies, even in a home setting. I say this because birth is not something that should be controlled in any way. If it is the wish of the woman giving birth that her partner should not attend, or if he himself does not feel entirely comfortable about being there, then he should not do so. In more traditional cultures women have always given birth in the company of other women. They still do. In these cultures, fathers are usually outside the room, but often nearby. There should be no rules about this. Women need to feel comfortable with whoever is in the room when they give birth. Ideally, the couple should decide attendance or non-attendance at the birth, but, ultimately, the decision has to rest with the woman giving birth because she is the one who needs to feel absolutely comfortable.

During labour and birth I believe that the father's importance is felt mainly through the mother. In other words, the child in the womb will only be aware of father's energy as it is transmitted to him via his mother. If she feels good and safe having him there, she will give birth with more ease. If on the other hand, his presence upsets mother then the baby will feel this through her.

IN THE HOSPITAL LABOUR ROOM

Does father have a place in the modern hospital labour room? Today, in most Western countries, fathers are expected to be present at the birth of their babies. However, with the increased medical management of birth the power of natural birth has been diluted and so, unfortunately, more often that not the father's role is to clean up the emotional mess that is created when the natural flow of birth is disturbed. Being present in a hospital labour room with its technological apparatus and machinery is not always easy. Sometimes the modern hospital labour room may look more like a torture chamber than a place of nature where a woman labours and where a child is about to be born.

It is difficult to feel at ease in a setting where technology has replaced nature. The father may feel useless and infantilised as he sees his partner hooked up to complicated machinery with information readings that only the staff can decipher. He may not be able to get near her, while she may feel frightened and in pain. He may feel intimidated by the medical and nursing attendants. He may be aware of her suffering and her frustration as she tries to get out of bed and onto her feet to ease her labour pains, and yet he may be powerless to help her. He may be appalled by the horrors he encounters in the labour room such as when his partner is cut so that the baby's head can be born. He may have to endure her heartrending screams as she is pulled apart by forceps and the baby is wrenched from her body; or when the epidural needle slips and she becomes damaged maybe for life. He may drift into quiet despair when the clock on the labour room wall moves from hour to hour and still there is no sign of the baby. His body may tighten with fear when he hears the doctors pronounce that they will have to carry out a caesarean section.

This sounds dramatic, and not all births in hospital are thus. However, in a hospital birth, especially if there is a 'problem', the father is often the lone figure in the corner of the room that people have forgotten about. In an emergency situation, he will have to deal with his own feelings of terror as he wonders whether his partner and the baby will make it. Suddenly the birth of the baby becomes a hazardous technological feat in which he has no part. Not wanting to be in the way, he sits quietly by as major decisions about his partner and his baby are made. Does he need to experience all this he wonders? Does he need to be there at all, since he doesn't appear to have a useful role? If on the other hand, the birth is natural and relatively trouble free, does he need to be there since nature will ensure that she will give birth without him anyway?

Men who have attended the birth of their children in hospital have described to me the different feelings they experienced. The more medicalised the birth, the more traumatic the feelings. One man spoke to me of his feelings of shock and horror as he stood by and witnessed his son's birth by forceps delivery. He was so appalled by the event, he vowed that if his wife and child came through it safely and intact, they would never again have another child. Another told me of the wrenching pain he felt, as he stood by helpless, while his partner screamed in agony. Yet another man said that he would remember forever the look in his wife's eyes as they wheeled her away to the operating theatre.

Some men have to cope with tumultuous and sometimes intolerable emotions while also containing them. There is no place for them to express these feelings. They are there to support and protect, so in a sense this also means that they have to hold a lot of their feelings back. That is just how it is.

Of course, not all hospital births are distressing or traumatic. Modern medical practitioners have become increasingly aware of the importance of combining the forces of nature with medical care while allowing the mother to give birth as naturally as possible. Fathers are being encouraged to play a more active role in the birth of their children. Nonetheless, hospitals are designed for the sick, not for normal healthy women giving birth.

LEFT OUT

In modern medicalised childbirth practice, it is easy for fathers to feel excluded, overlooked or marginalised. If a particular father has any conscious or unconscious feelings of inferiority or insecurity in relation to his capacity to be a father, medicalised childbirth may certainly exacerbate things. He may feel he has no part to play in the process, and that he must leave it to the 'experts'. This makes it harder for him to feel connected to the joy of the experience.

A traumatic birth experience will be all the more difficult for the father to take when contrasted with the months of pregnancy when he witnessed the unfolding bloom of life and heard his child's quiet heartbeat. Labour, followed by the birth of his baby may shock him into a rude awakening of his fatherhood. If this is the couple's first child, the event will shake them; it will change the status quo; it will bring reality in with a bang. If his partner has previously been the strong one in the relationship, then her emotional and physical vulnerability at this time may alarm him. He may not feel ready for responsibility or capable of handling it. He may find himself having to take care of many more tasks than previously, and his lifestyle will change. It is during the birth itself and in the weeks following it that the full reality of fatherhood finally dawns on him.

DEALING WITH THE FEELINGS

The birth of a child is a powerful archetypal experience. It will most certainly bring up as many feelings for the father as it does for the mother, though in a different way. In my experience of working with couples during childbirth, fathers deal with the powerful feelings aroused by the birth in somewhat diverse ways. Some men were so in tune with the overall process that during the labour and birth it felt as if we were all one; there were no gender differences in the room. Their anima was so much in evidence, these men flowed with the process and this enhanced the women's task of giving birth. Still others were able to hold and support their partners all the way through the labour and the birth itself without either interfering or opting out. When this happened, the labouring woman relaxed into the birth process much more easily. Some however, finding the arduous and sometimes prolonged labour of their partners stressful, took refuge in withdrawal or irritable behaviour that added to the difficulties.

How a father deals with the powerful feelings aroused in him during childbirth will affect the mother. From my experience of being with couples during labour, I can say that even the subtlest emotions in the father caused changes in the atmosphere. I felt tangible shifts in energy that had to do with how he was coping. A labouring woman will literally open to the love and support she feels from her partner. She feels everything and senses everything because in the energy of birth, she is open to all energetic influences no matter how subtle. If her partner is fearful, she will pick it up and she may want to protect him. Alternatively, sensing his fear, she may be angry with him for letting her down. She may not feel entirely free to follow the dictates of her body, which draw her deep into her sexual and instinctual nature. Some fathers are irritable and short tempered with the stress of long, sleepless hours and continuing cries of pain from the mother as she tries to cope with the exhaustion of a protracted labour.

I recall one occasion when a labouring woman asked me to take her husband out of the room. She was exhausted after almost 24 hours in labour, but she still wanted to hold out for a natural birth and so refused pain relief. He was distraught and could not cope with her cries of pain; he wanted her to take pain-relieving medication. It was clear there was friction between them, and this was preventing her from relaxing into her labour. We walked around the hospital together while he smoked cigarettes and let off steam. When we returned after half an hour, her labour had progressed, and she had dilated by three centimetres!

TUNING IN

In my experience, the nature of a couple's relating, especially their sexual relationship, is revealed in the way they interact during the labour and birth. As already stated, birth is such an intensely physical experience, a natural extension of sexual relating, that it arouses strong emotions in those present. If both partners are comfortable in their individual and their joint sexuality, then the process of labour and birth flows more freely. A man who is grounded in his body and in his own sexual nature will be able to support his partner simply by being present in the birth room. The instinctual nature of birth will not frighten or daunt him. He will be comfortable with the sights and sounds of a birthing mother. Similarly, if their relationship is sound and their sexual energies flow well together, then his energy will support her and she will be able to let go. It is a very subtle process, and it has nothing to do with verbal expression. Rather it is an intuitive body language, a connection to the blood of life; bone deep experience.

I recall an interesting example of this some time ago. It had nothing to do with the actual birth of a baby, but in essence it was the same type of experience. I was speaking to a large group of people at the launch of my book. I was speaking about birth, about the spiritual nature of birth and the loss of soul that occurs when technology interferes with the natural flow of energy in labour. My partner was with me, quietly sitting to one side. He was in charge of the book selling. As a graphic artist he had also designed the front cover of the book and the publicity material relating to it. He is a father, but he is not otherwise involved in the process of childbirth in any way. During my talk, which went extremely well, I was very aware of his quiet presence. Although unobtrusive, I could actually feel his birth energy glowing. It supported me, and it helped me to flow with what I had to do that evening. Having begun my talk feeling tired after an extremely long journey, I now found myself relaxing completely into my work. You could hear a pin drop such was the degree of oneness and attention in the room. I felt inspired. Elated, I could have gone on speaking all night. We talked about it later. I believe it was his innate and grounded birth energy that came to the fore that evening. It was also his commitment and love both for me and the work that we were doing together. I felt it and it helped me. It was truly soul work.

If a man can stand in reverence before a process in which he does not actively have to take part, then he allows something to flow. He enhances it simply by his presence. That is all that is required. Fathers, who are very involved in the birth of their babies such as at a home birth, report feelings of awe at the power of nature at work. Many of them instinctively know where to be and what to do.

One man spoke of his awe at the power of his partner's birthing of their son at home. 'It was awesome. Sandy was so clear and in her power. It was beyond strength and definition. It just was. I was seriously impressed to see nature at work in this way. It was beyond the personal. I wished to experience myself at this level of proficiency. What initiation does life offer men for a similar potential experience?

BEING THERE

Modern life does not offer men any experience that can equal giving birth as an act of initiation. In fact, in the birth process the archetypal roles of men and women switch. The father cannot give birth; he has simply to flow with the process. He has to be in his feminine energy, receptive and containing, without the need to take action. Like my partner on the evening of my talk, he must simply be there and let his love flow freely from an open heart so as to help or facilitate his partner. Conversely, the mother, who is actively giving birth, is in her masculine at this time, particularly in the second stage of her labour. She is involved in an intensely physical task; it is very hard 'work'. She moves with the power in her body, while he waits and does nothing. It is an interesting juxtaposition of power and balance.

It is a strange quirk of nature that in order to empower herself to give birth, a woman must call on her masculine and feminine energies to join forces. She is drawing on both her instinctive, female nature, and her active masculine energy. In actual fact they are indistinguishable, for our generative natures contain both a male and female aspect. In births where women endure a high degree of medical intervention, it is common for them to report feeling profoundly disempowered. This feeling is particularly common with instrumental births such as delivery by forceps. Not being able to push their own baby out causes them to feel loss of potency. They feel wounded in their instinctual abilities.

As I said, our generative natures contain both a masculine and a feminine aspect. The masculine enlists the feminine. They work together. This is the basis of all creative acts. Awareness of this fact is vitally important when examining the father's role in childbirth, which is essentially receptive. The problem lies in the fact that it is not always understood that both men and women have masculine and feminine aspects and that men can be in their feminine, receptive and nurturing. This way of being is not by and large validated in men, neither is it validated by men, women or society as a whole. Men are expected to 'do' rather than simply 'be'. If men could learn that they have a real value in 'being without doing', and if women could allow them that freedom, then I believe we would be closer to achieving a balance in the male/female dynamic. As women we usually project 'animus' onto our men and we expect them to 'do'. We really do need to value them in their being.

COACHING FATHERS

I believe that generally it is a good thing for fathers to be present at the birth of their children. However, as previously stated, I would not advocate this in every case. I would not make it a rule. In an ideal world all births would take place at home or in a home-like environment where both partners can participate in the event. There, the father's presence is less apt to be questioned because he is in his own house. His role as protector or guardian is facilitated. In a hospital setting things are different. Here the father's true role has yet to be properly defined. To avoid being merely an onlooker at the birth of his own child, he needs to be invited to participate in whatever way is deemed most appropriate to both partners.

When I ran the Holistic Birth Centre, I would encourage the man to be the spokesperson for the labouring mother. He would be familiar with the birth plan they had drawn up prior to the birth, which incorporated his partner's wishes about pain relief and medical intervention. He would protect her from the intrusive gazes and interventions of the birth attendants if he considered they were bothering her. He, rather than she, would discuss things with nurses and doctors if medical interventions appeared necessary. He would take up the position as his labouring partner's prime supporter. This would leave her free to get on with the task of giving birth. He might massage her back; prepare snacks and drinks, or mop her brow if she needed him to. He would be attentive to her every need, listening out for her. He would be a soothing presence in a strange place. Usually, he was the only person the labouring women knew in a place of strangers.

In order to be able to 'be there' as effectively as possible, most fathers needed some 'coaching' from me in how to deal with the medical side of things. They needed to be informed of their rights vis-à-vis the hospital and medical procedures. In Britain it was, and still is the case, that no action or procedure can be carried out by the hospital staff on a labouring woman without her informed consent. This is the type of information that helped the father to become more assertive with the medical attendants if he felt it was necessary. I always reminded fathers (and mothers) that this was their baby and their birth! A simple thing you might say, but it is surprising the number of people who become infantilised as soon as they enter a hospital environment. Believing that the hospital staff are the 'experts, even in something as natural as childbirth, many people will put aside their own inner knowledge and succumb to painful or invasive procedures that are not always necessary.

The couple will have learnt in the prenatal classes at the Birth Centre, what each medical procedure entailed as well as their risks and benefits. They will have learnt about the various forms of medical pain relief likely to be offered. They will have been aware that they could exercise choice in the way they wanted their child to be born. They will also, as a couple, have practised a variety of different exercises and yoga type postures to help with natural pain relief. They will have learnt what positions to adopt in labour and how to support the mother in a squatting position while giving birth. They will have become familiar with the breathing exercises that facilitate flowing with the pain of contractions, and what positions to adopt for the most effective delivery of the baby.

Usually, if a couple had prepared well and the expectant

mother had come regularly to the prenatal yoga classes, they were ready for the birth of their child. Of course, some parents despite preparation still ended up with a very medicalised birth. But again, if they were included in all decisions, this did not result in them feeling disempowered. For others who felt pushed around and badly treated, the birth of their child left a bitter mark on their souls. Unless they sought therapy, afterwards, they tended not to have a forum where they could express these feelings. For fathers the situation was often worse because generally they protected their partners by not expressing their pain and simply buried the strong feelings.

Despite my role as prenatal and birth teacher, it is not possible to 'coach' a mother to give birth any more than it is possible to 'coach' a father to 'be there'. I have written about this in greater detail in my last book. It is sufficient to say that in the context of this book, women in childbirth need the firm and solid commitment of their partners. Men need to feel they have a role and can play a useful part in the process of birth. Below I have included some pointers which fathers in childbirth may find useful. These can be used as reference both in preparation for and during labour.

A WORKBOOK FOR FATHERS DURING CHILDBIRTH

Pregnancy

- Attend some or all of the prenatal classes designed for couples.
- Practise yoga positions so that you can help physically support your partner in labour and during birth.
- Read some of her books if you feel the need to be better informed about the changes taking place in your partner due to her pregnancy, and if you want to find out what to expect in childbirth.
- Become aware of your feelings. Meditate or find time to do some reflective work with your inner soul. Allow into your awareness your feelings about becoming a father. Be aware of any fears, anxieties or expectations

that you might have about your partner's labour and the forthcoming birth of your child.

- Talk to other men with children who have attended births.
- Try to remain open to your partner's needs and expectations of you. She may be emotionally labile and her needs will change.
- Look after the practical side of your life together as much as you can
- If there are other children, remember to give them attention too.
- Be as involved as you can be with her pregnancy. Listen to the baby's heartbeat as soon as you can. Talk, recite poetry or sing to the baby if you wish.
- Massage or stroke her pregnant body if she likes this. The baby will sense it.
- Keep your heart and your arms open.
- Be there. If you are not fully committed she will feel it. So will the child.

LABOUR AND BIRTH

Hospital

- Become informed about all likely medical procedures and pain relief measures that are likely to be offered.
- Make sure you are aware of your partner's needs and wishes in relation to labour.
- Make a birth plan with her well in advance of her due date. Make sure it is discussed with the doctor and/or the labour ward staff and attached to her notes.
- Visit the labour ward in advance if possible.
- On arrival at the hospital check the room and make it as comfortable as possible in accordance with her needs and wishes.
- Bring items such as music tapes, camera, drinks and snacks if desired. Many hospitals don't allow women to eat during labour, but a flask of hot water and a jar of honey are useful for making a sweet drink. This helps to maintain blood sugar levels during labour.
- Bring light scented water such as rosewater to spray

on her face and a flannel to wipe her brow; lip salve for dry lips, fresh or bottled water; Arnica and other home opathic remedies if desired.

- In your dealings with the birth attendants, become the spokesperson for your partner as soon as you can. Be assertive and confident about what you want without being aggressive. Listen to the pros and cons of any procedures offered, and try to arrive at a balanced decision between you. Remember to be flexible.
- Protect your partner and prevent anyone who upsets her from entering the room. Also prevent too many people coming in.
- Protect her from distracting noise or chatter.
- If she wants you there, make sure you stay close to her.
- Let her cry or express her birthing pain as freely as she wishes.
- Encourage her to breathe deeply and hold her if she wishes.
- Try not to be afraid of her pain.
- Remember to breathe yourself!
- Just be there. Don't feel you have to do anything.
- Trust your intuition
- Help her into a sitting, standing or squatting position during labour, and for delivery of the baby, if this is what she wants. The baby will come more quickly in an upright position because the pelvis can open more and the child moves down with the force of gravity.
- Try and facilitate as gentle a birth as possible for the baby, with low lights and no loud noises for example.
- After the birth, try to ensure that the baby is put directly onto your partner's tummy. If this is not possible, then ask to hold the baby yourself.
- Encourage the baby to suck at the breast as soon as possible
- Stay centred, calm and hold the energy for your partner and the baby if there is an emergency or a medical problem
- If you feel very stressed, anxious or upset take a break outside the room.
- Don't be afraid to let your feelings flow after the birth. Give in to tears if this is what comes up for you.

- Keep your heart open.
- Be there without feeling you have to do anything.
- Enjoy

AT HOME

- Take care of all the practical things like making sure in advance that the car has petrol in it for example, just in case you need to go to the hospital.
- Be well informed in advance about how your partner wants to give birth and what she needs.
- If you are planning to be at the birth make sure that you feel secure and confident with her choices. If you are afraid, she will sense it.
- Prepare the space or the room where your partner is planning to give birth. Fill the birth pool for example. Turn on music if she has chosen to have some. Light candles.
- Keep the room warm.
- Make sure the other children in the house are looked after.
- Protect your partner from intrusions such as a ringing phone or doorbell, or unnecessary callers.
- Make sure she has everything she needs to give birth naturally and easily.
- Breathe and encourage her to breathe. Support her in yoga positions and upright posture if that is what she has chosen. Massage her if that is what she wants.
- Encourage her to go with the force of nature. Don't be afraid of her expressions of pain. Let her groan or cry.
- Keep calm and remember that she only needs you to 'be present'.
- Stay in your centre and use your intuition about when, if at all, to act.
- 'Be there' as fully and as completely as you can.
- After the birth, hold her and the baby as soon as you possibly can.
- Let your own feelings flow after the baby is born.
- Keep your heart open
- Enjoy

A FEW DON'TS

- Don't panic!
- Don't tell her what to do unless she asks your advice.
- Don't lose faith in her ability to give birth even if she is distressed.
- Don't suggest pain relief when you are already aware that she wants to avoid it. Let her decide when and if she wants it.
- When and if she loses faith in her ability to give birth, encourage her.
- Don't DO anything unless it is obvious that some action on your part is needed
- Don't withdraw emotionally.

CHAPTER THREE

FATHER IN THE NURSERY

Your children are not your children.
They are the sons and daughters of Life's
longing for itself.
They come through you but not from you,
And though they are with you yet they belong
Not to you.

(The Prophet, Kahlil Gibran)

Up until fairly recently psychological thought was that fathers only became important in a child's life after infancy. More recent research into the psychology of child development however, indicates that male children in particular have a great need for their fathers in the first two years of their lives. Studies indicate that male children who have absent fathers during the first two years of their existence are more likely to develop psychological problems.[1] Boys whose fathers were absent for long periods of time, or who had gone away when they were very young showed deficiencies on social, sexual, moral and cognitive levels. These studies also suggested that boys who experienced father absence before the age of two were more affected than those boys who experienced father absence at a later age. Less work has been done on the importance of the father to the development of girls, but common sense and psychology indicates that the father is an important figure in a child's life from the very beginning.

The first few days and weeks after a baby's birth can be a trying time, particularly for first time parents. When I was involved in prenatal teaching many couples, especially mothers told me that despite prenatal courses, they did not feel really prepared for the upheaval in their lives following the birth of their babies. The reality of the demands of caring for a new baby can be daunting. The mother will be recovering physically and emotionally from the powerful experience of giving birth. Now in addition, she has a tiny infant totally dependent on her. She will probably be getting little sleep and her body will be unsettled due to the huge upsurge of hormones. The father will have to get used to the upheaval in his home and normal routine. The arrival of his tiny child will stir all sorts of feelings in him. His partner may be withdrawn and irritable as well as preoccupied with caring for the baby. Both partners will have to adjust to their new lives as parents. For them, the postnatal period will be a time of major change. How they cope with it will depend on many factors.

THE BLUES

A short period of depression or what is usually called the 'blues' is very common in postnatal women. This may alarm the father. There is no need to be alarmed at the blues since this short burst of depression soon passes. If the birth of the baby has been difficult however, and the mother becomes depressed as a result, the father may find it difficult to cope. He might find it hard to understand why his partner is depressed. The child is healthy. She is healthy. What reason could there be for the blues?

The birth of a child is meant to be a joyous event and in most cases it is. However, childbirth can occasionally result in postnatal depression. Sometimes this depression can be severe. I have written about this at length in my last book. However, I do not think much has been written about the effect that a partner's postnatal depression can have on the father of the child. In my experience, fathers, quite naturally, find postnatal depression very difficult to cope with. Like most depressions, unless you are experiencing it, it is difficult to relate to. You are shut out from the person who has withdrawn. Unless you have been depressed yourself at some stage in your life, you will not know how it feels to wake up every morning under a black cloud and want to go back to sleep again.

In my view, depression is often nature's way of alerting you to something that needs to be dealt with. It is a cry from the soul. A depression is a minor initiation and occurs most frequently during times of transition. Childbirth is a huge transition and it will bring up a lot of previously hidden feelings and unresolved conflicts from childhood. These will be loosened during the birth and afterwards. Responsibility and caring for your newborn baby will draw you back to many incidents a time long ago when you were a baby. Your new baby's cries will tug at your heart in such a way that you will be drawn to what still needs healing in your soul. This will happen unbeknownst to you. Your inner child will wake up when your own child is born, and if it is wounded it will claim your attention. You will not recognise yourself in the cries or the laughter of your child, but you will be there nonetheless.

For fathers, the depression of their partners after childbirth will be challenging. It generally creates in them huge feelings of helplessness. They don't know what to do. They feel powerless. If they are unused to dealing with these feelings, a sense of helplessness will make them angry or irritated. They may send their partner off to the doctor for prescription drugs and may feel better if their illness is 'labelled' postnatal depression. This makes it somehow more bearable or understandable as depression becomes something that you catch, like a virus.

The modern tendency to medicalise problems of the heart and soul means that we are inclined to dissociate ourselves from our own inner voices and from responsibility for our own health. This exacerbates things further. A father may be in denial of his own latent depressive feelings, and he may therefore project these onto his partner. Or he may feel inadequate and unable to relate to his wife's recent emotional neediness. He may then withdraw which will push her even further away.

Francie's wife got postnatal depression after the birth of their eldest son. She was withdrawn and unhappy, had no energy and showed little interest in the baby. Francie did not know what to do. He could not relate to her emotionally. He was no good at feelings, he told me. He sent her off to their GP and she was put on anti-depressant drugs, which meant she could not breastfeed their son. Although she recovered eventually and came off the drugs, she remained tired and lethargic and, it seemed, was always on the verge of becoming depressed again. Their relationship became distant and sometimes fraught since Francie's wife was in need of emotional support and he could not give it. After years of struggle, (some of which were spent in couples therapy), and following the birth of their second child, they finally split up.

When Francie came to see me many years later, following the failure of two further relationships with 'depressed' women, I began to see that he had never resolved his own unconscious feelings of depression. He was a 'fair weather' person who tended to run a mile from any unpleasant emotion such as depression, pain or grief. In his choice of partners could be detected a need to come to terms with his own latent depression. He had never mourned the loss of his mother who died when he was a teenager. The birth of his own son and his wife's subsequent depression led him to a precarious place. Internally, Francie feared falling apart. He feared he might break down if he were to let himself feel too much.

It became clear that some of his wife's depression was actually his, for it is in the nature of things that we meet and encounter aspects of ourselves out there in other people. His inner world, if he had allowed himself to go there, was ravaged with loss. On the outside however, he was sunny and confident. Francie had been brought up to hide his feelings and to keep a 'stiff upper lip' at all times. To acknowledge the ravaged nature of his inner world would be to open up a can of worms. He was shielded by a coat of armour to which he had grown accustomed. If challenged however, he would deny it existed and so he kept his incipient depression at bay. His wife, and later his girlfriends, carried or embodied his depressions for him.

INNER CHILD

The birth of his child will bring up for the father all kinds of other feelings from his own childhood. Some of these may be expressed unconsciously in the way he reacts to his wife after the birth of their baby. He may be angry with his wife for being depressed and withdrawn, especially if his relationship with his own mother was complicated by feelings of rejection and abandonment. In his little child's newborn cries and his wife's preoccupation he may relive the emptiness of his childhood years when his needs were not met. If, on the other hand, she throws herself fully into her mothering role and meets the very challenging demands of her newborn baby, he may experience quite a different set of reactions. He may feel left out. If he is nursing a mother wound somewhere in his heart, then he may even resent the attention she gives to the baby. His child then becomes his competitor in a strange but powerful way, obscuring his ability to parent the child. One young father told me he remembered looking at his wife's beautiful breasts as she prepared to feed their baby and felt envious of the child. He wondered if they would they ever belong to him again. He would not allow the feeling to be described as jealousy, but it was there nonetheless.

A father needs to be very secure both internally and in his wife's affections in order not to feel a bit threatened by the birth of his child, especially if the child is a son. A defenceless newborn will bring up the strongest feelings of vulnerability and tenderness in both men and women. The baby's very dependency will stir up unwanted memories of being vulnerable at the hands of the more powerful parent. If the father has internalised being loved as a child, then he will glow with love for his own child. His love will flow as his heart expands to feed his child the love he feels for it. If he has had a good experience of being mothered and fathered, then he will feel confident in his abilities and role as a father. If on the other hand, he lacked a strong father, then he may imagine he is without the resources necessary to father and he feels himself to be inadequate. And so the birth may push him into an uncomfortable place where he fears the responsibility placed upon him and he longs secretly to flee. Indeed, some very insecure fathers do flee because they are fearful of the finality of the commitment that the birth of a child means for them.

This is what happened to Martin. Having had been brought up solely by his mother, he was a man who had a huge father hunger of which he was unaware. Conceived as a result of a brief liaison, he had never met his father and knew little about him. He believed him to be dead. When Martin was scarcely more than a teenager he fathered a child with a casual girlfriend. Horrified, he ran away from the situation. He never acknowledged the child, running as far as he could from any notion of the responsibility of fatherhood. He was still looking for his own father; how could he be a father himself? In the strange way that life has of drawing us to the place of hurt, history had repeated itself.

In his early 30s Martin's partner got pregnant unexpectedly and again, he recoiled from his impending fatherhood.

The child was aborted. The relationship broke up. By the time I met him, Martin was living with a woman who had two children from a previous relationship. Whether they should have a child of their own and his feelings about it were the focus of the first year of his therapy. Although he had run from fatherhood, his soul pulled him to heal his father wound through becoming a parent himself.

It is not often that fathers prepare psychologically for the experience of becoming a father, but this in effect was what happened with Martin. When he came to understand his own father hunger, and began to heal the emptiness and pain caused by his early lack of fathering, he ceased to run from the prospect of fatherhood. Two years after starting therapy, he became the proud father of a son.

BECOMING A FATHER:
HEALING THE BOY

For other men lack of fathering in their own childhoods creates a strong desire to do things very differently when they become fathers. A man who was inadequately fathered vows to give his child everything he didn't have. In the fathering of his own child, an unfathered man can heal his father wound. This will be particularly evident in the way he fathers his sons. Sometimes it happens that an estranged son will be motivated to heal a rift with his father when he himself becomes a father. In becoming a father he has the chance to resolve unfinished childhood injuries or traumas. He may see his father in a new light and begin to understand him.

Matthew was estranged from his father. He had not seen him since his father had left home during the bitter break-up of his parents' marriage. Matthew was a hurt little boy of twelve who dealt with his feelings of abandonment and betrayal at the hands of his father by cutting him out of his life. All attempts by his father to reach him were rebuffed. It was many years later, as he held his own newborn baby in his arms and looked down into his son's eyes, that he began to think of forgiving his father. Something huge shifted and moved in his chest as he held his son. Years of repressed pain were unleashed and a healing started there and then as he recalled clearly his father's face bending over his own small one, 30 years before. He softened and began to think about reconciling with his father, now a man advancing into old age. The birth of his own son brought him not only fatherhood, but also his own father.

John, on the other hand, longed to give his sons the fathering he didn't have. His own lack of fathering means he could not trust himself as a father. His fathering, like his inner world, is disorganised and erratic. On certain occasions he behaves as if he suddenly remembers that he is a father and pulls at the thin vestiges of fathering left him by his own father. Not finding it sufficient to ground him, he has to draw on the tenuous and elusive legacy of fatherhood as fed him from an outdated military type patriarchy. When his sons were small, he became fanatical and strict about relatively trivial things such as table manners, forgetting the more substantial things that a boy's soul needs from his father if he is to become a confident man. Often, he failed his sons and disappointed them, even though this was not his intention. Since he secretly felt inadequate as a father, he was a remote, somewhat forbidding figure, and this pushed them into a place of hunger. In the day-to-day struggle of fathering however, a wounded father if he sticks at it, will find his fathering ability. His sons will reflect it to him.

Joe remembers waiting anxiously for his father to come home on a specific evening each week so that they could all sit down together to watch a particular television programme. It was the highlight of the week for him. It meant a lot to have his father there, since he was often away. In his own way, Joe was teaching his father how to be a father. He needed him there. Joe like other boys needed to connect with the very physicality of his father so that he could grow into a strong man secure in his own masculinity.

JOCASTA'S CHILDREN

Sometimes a father is prevented from having a more intimate relationship with his children because their mother is unconsciously creating a barrier between them. In our modern world where fathers are generally out at work for long hours each day and children are left to the sole care of their mother this barrier is more prevalent than one would like to think. French psychoanalyst Christiane Olivier's book *Jocasta's Children; The Imprint of the Mother* examines the whole notion of the power of the mother to hold her children captive and, more significantly, to create a distance between them and their father. This book highlights the conspiracy not just between mothers and sons, but also between mothers and their children.

In Greek mythology Jocasta was the mother of Oedipus and the wife of Laius. Jocasta unknowingly married her son Oedipus and bore him children after the death of Laius. As the title 'Jocasta's children' implies, the mother's stronghold is incestuously tinged. She claims her children and most especially if her relationship with the father is not good, she will often use them to further her own ends by enlisting them in her battle with their father. Because her controlling energy is subtle and intangible, her power will be only vaguely recognised as such by those caught up in its web. As Olivier points out, babies and very small children are generally cared for by their mothers and they are totally at her mercy since during this time in their lives their vulnerability is at its peak. A mother may unwittingly do psychological damage to her baby by creating subtle physical and emotional bonds that could be considered incestuous in that they are in fact more appropriate for her relationship with her partner. Adult desire mixes uneasily with infantile instinctive feelings and urges.

The child's psychological welfare may easily get lost in the desire of the mother. We can see this with Marc who for many years slept with his mother while his father slept in the next room. We will be meeting Mark later in the book. I thought about this again when a man told me in a therapy session that his mother had made frequent references to his dainty figure and golden curly hair when he was a little boy. She would admire him saying that 'with looks like that you should have been a girl!' This had confused him, and it gave him mixed messages about his gender identity, which affected his sexual orientation later on in life.

In the case of another of my clients Nicola, it was quite evident that for as far back as she could remember, she was lifted from her own little bed in the middle of the night and placed in her parents' bed by her mother. She became the excuse her mother used to avoid sexually relating to her husband. Nicola grew up as the go-between, and her young heart was filled with anxieties and fears about her parents. At one stage she even slept with a knife under her pillow, ready to defend her mother when her father came in drunk, and the arguing would start. As an adult she was beset with panic attacks and phobias. In therapy she told me that she was afraid to fall asleep. She feared that her father might kill her mother.

Nicola was a Jocasta's child. Her mother claimed her. Later on in life she longed to have a relationship with her father but instead she projected this deep father hunger onto the men she chose as partners. They were invariably older men. Her mother's bitterness and complicated feelings of anger and desire in relation to her husband in particular and men in general sat uneasily with Nicola's naturally loving nature. It confused her. It made her relationships with men and women complicated. She had great difficulty breaking free of her mother. Her guilt at what she perceived as her abandonment of her mother constantly pulled her back. She wanted a relationship with 'father,' with the masculine, but doing so meant abandoning mother and the feminine. She could not reach her own father, who had long since separated from her mother, a quiet reclusive man.

And Mark also bears the scars of being a Jocasta's child. He was his mother's secret lover when he was barely old enough to walk. As an adult man he still carries a hidden fear of women and yet he desires them. His bonds with his mother confuse and complicate his relationships.

When Jocasta claims her children she taints them; she turns them in a subtle way against their own father and in doing so she inflicts on them a wound that is difficult to heal.

Sometimes the mother claims her children in a much more subtle way. All children pick up the imponderables in their parents' souls, especially their mothers' souls. They are aware of their mother's thoughts and feelings. Of her disappointments, her fears and her anxieties. If her heart is disappointed and disillusioned with her partner and perhaps with the love ideal, they will sense it. Children know somewhere in their being the whole story of their parents and their relationship. A mother's disappointment with father often communicates itself in such a way that it results in the child drawing closer to her and further from father. The child will not be aware of taking sides in the conflict between his parents until perhaps many years later. But he will have been drawn in nontheless, and his soul will know this whilst his psyche will retain the scars of this time.

MOTHER'S POWER

Most mothers exercise great power over the emotional lives of their children simply because usually, it is the mother who reigns supreme in the nursery. In a bad marriage or relationship where the mother is continually 'put down' or disregarded by father, it is easier for her to claim her power through her children. Such a mother may become controlling and possessive of her children.

In other cases, such as where a mother and father are involved in a destructive or even violent relationship, it is not uncommon for the children to be used as ammunition. I recall one instance where Rosie, a mother of five who had regularly been the subject of abuse and violence at the hands of her husband, found that she vented all her pent up rage on her ten-year-old son. Rosie was the mother of four girls and one boy by two different fathers. She had been the victim of violence at the hands of the fathers of her children. She had now left her marriage and was embarking on a course of therapy. Although a compassionate and aware woman who loved her children, under stress she often lashed out against her son. This appalled her. She sought to understand the basis of her frustration and why she felt compelled to punish him.

In the course of our sessions she became aware that in a way she was acting out her huge need for positive contact with the masculine. Her negative experience of the masculine meant that she had profound unresolved feelings towards men and she needed to heal these. Her son embodied the male for her. In him at times she saw the male energy that his father had used to abuse her. She also saw in him the tender boy whom she needed to protect. At a deeper level still, her son represented a complicated mixture of desire, love and hate. She was very angry with men because she had been the victim of their brutality yet at the same time she wanted to love them and to follow her natural instincts. With this complicated mixture of emotions, Rosie experienced great internal conflict.

RECLAIMING FATHER

The Oedipus myth is based on an absent father. The father can mitigate the power of the mother in the nursery. Perhaps such abuses as described above would not have happened had the fathers been strong and actively present in their children's lives. A child needs its father's as well as its mother's energy. Fathers who are involved with the daily care of their babies and young children report a closer bond and a more intimate relationship with them later on. Changing and bathing their babies offers fathers the opportunity to play with and be intimate with their children. And children, as we have seen, benefit hugely from this physical and emotional closeness.

That said, father's presence is needed in a different way to that of the mother. His is perhaps a more ephemeral energy at first, which is introduced gradually and with increasing intensity as the child grows away from the cocoon of his perinatal and childhood years. Father's energy really comes into action for the child when he helps the child out of his dependency with his mother. It is the father's energy that helps the child negotiate his or her place in the world.

I write about reclaiming father because often he is not considered an important figure in a baby and a very young child's life. As I said earlier, this is erroneous thinking. Increasingly, we are learning not only about the great awareness that babies and children have quite naturally, we are also learning about the positive and negative effects that a father's presence can have in a child's life. Today, there are too many stories of fatherless children who grow up with problems. Boys in particular have been shown over and over again, to need the firm hand of a father in order to grow into secure, confident and positive men.

Of course, for many children, both boys and girls, the strong and loving presence of both a mother and a father is not a given. Children lose parents through death, divorce and other life events, and there are many mothers bringing up children single-handedly who do an excellent job. And women today can even choose to have children without the active presence of a father. Many of these children grow into confidant and secure adults. However, an awareness of the impor-

tance of father, of father's energy to the child is very important. A mother who brings up a child alone needs to hold the
awareness of the gap left by an absent father. A fatherless
child may find the father energy he or she needs in other close
male relatives and later on, in teachers and friends. Ensuring
that this is made possible is very important.

Notes

1. H. Biller, Fatherhood: *Implications for Child and Adult Development.*
    Ed. Woolman, B. pp711-714

CHAPTER FOUR

THE FATHER'S BIRTH GIFT

"The father gives with his sperm a black overcoat around the soul, invisible in our black nights. He gave and gives a sheathing, or envelope, or coating around the soul made entirely of intensity, shrewdness, desire to penetrate, liveliness, impulse, daring. The father's birth gift cannot be quantified. It has something to do with love of knowledge, love of the mind, and a way to honor the world of things."

(Robert Bly in Mothers/Fathers)

These words express something of the energy of the father. What a father brings to his child is very different to what a mother brings. What is the father's birth gift? The father's gift is not closeness. Most mythology refers to the father as an authoritarian and somewhat distant figure, no less important than the mother, but with a very different formative energy. His influence is perceived and felt through different channels. Father or the masculine principle calls to us through a different part of our souls. The masculine and the feminine, father and mother are complimentary. Ideally, a child should have both a mother and a father when it comes into the world. Together they add up to wholeness. We need both male and female aspects within us in order to be harmonious and in balance. The soul seeks wholeness above all else.

It used to be that the father's role in a child's life was not considered to have anything near the importance of the mother's. Mother was all-important, an understandable view given that it is the mother who conceives, nurtures and gives birth to the child. David Kay, Jungian analyst and author writes of this 'absence' in psychological literature suggesting that further investigation of father/infant psychology and psychopathology is important for clinical work[1]. Certainly I believe that whereas in clinical practice psychological eyes have tended to focus on the influence of the mother in early life and infancy, it is now necessary, especially in our current climate, to focus on the father's influence.

There is a lot of evidence to suggest that where there is an absence of father, there is a void. This void may be expressed in many ways, but one of the most common is confusion and chaos. I have found this more particularly when working therapeutically with men. Unfathered men veer towards confusion, and in times of stress or vulnerability they can become very disordered, uncertain and uncentred. Perhaps this is because one of the father's birth gifts is order. We will come back to this when we look in more detail at the father's role in the formation of his child. Jung's paper *'The significance of the Father in the destiny of the individual'*[2] underlines the importance of the father. In my clinical practice I have been much influenced by his work and that of later Jungian analysts and authors such as the aforementioned Robert Bly, Jim Fitzgerald and Guy Corneau.

GOD THE FATHER

All infants and small children begin by regarding their parents as Gods, or sometimes, Kings and Queens. People with tremendous power. This is a very necessary thing for a child. As Jung writes 'The parental imago is possessed of quite an extraordinary power; it influences the psychic life of the child so enormously that we must ask ourselves whether we may attribute such magnitude to an ordinary human being at all'. Of course Jung was at this time developing his theory of archetypes. Behind the personal mother and father lie the archetypes of the mother and father. Archetypes are universal principles, ideas and images or forces that influence us. Archetypes are inherited and are 'in potential' in each child, so that by the time a child is born there is already present in him or her the very 'idea' of parents. He or she is primed to 'expect' to be parented. Parents are part of a child's archetypal inheritance.

Jung describes it thus 'Man possesses many things which he has never acquired but has inherited from his ancestors.

He is not born a 'tabula rasa' he is merely born unconscious. But he brings with him systems that are organised and ready to function in a specifically human way, and these he owes to millions of years of human development. Just as the migratory and nest-building instincts of birds were never learnt or acquired individually, man brings with him at birth the ground plan of his nature, and not only of his individual nature but of his collective nature. These inherited systems correspond to the human situations that have existed since primeval times: youth and old age, birth and death, sons and daughters, fathers and mothers, mating and so on. I have called this congenital and pre-existent instinctual model, or pattern of behaviour, the archetype'.[3]

So, a child is born knowing. He knows about many things. Even if there is no father present, the child will have some kind of inner knowing about fathers and he will feel a lack. He may not be aware of what is lacking, but unconsciously he will try and find ways to fill it. He will draw on other things and people to clothe a skeleton father. For, you could say that the archetype is a skeleton waiting to be given flesh. An archetype is drawn into human life and activated through experience. In other words, life experience clothes and gives form to the archetype. In this way the father archetype, for example, is humanised through the personal father. So the child learns about the father, he learns what this dim or indistinct feeling of father is through his experience of relating to his own father. This is what we mean when we talk about humanising the archetype. All of us need to have the archetype of the mother and the father humanised and embodied in our own parents in order to feel our way into life as secure human beings. The less a mother or father is 'present' to humanise the archetype for us, the more influence the (disembodied) archetype will have on our psyches, making it harder for us to incarnate as human beings.

We all need guidance. If we remember that we are souls clothed in a human body rather than human bodies with a soul, then it makes sense that coming from the spirit world, we need guidance on being human, on taking human form. If the guidance is not evident then we may lose our way. The child is guided by the power of his parents as by a higher destiny. This makes sense if we remember that the child possesses an inherited system that anticipates the existence of parents and their influence upon him. In other words, behind the father lies the father archetype, and in this pre-existent archetype lies the secret of the father's power, just as the power that forces the bird to migrate is not produced by the bird itself but derives from its ancestors. The personal father inevitably embodies the archetype. The archetype acts as an amplifier, enhancing beyond measure the effects that proceed from the father, insofar as these conform to the inherited pattern. What guidance does the father bring to his child? In the following paragraphs I have drawn together various writings, mainly Jungian influenced. Jung's own writings on the significance of the father are interwoven with my own thoughts and clinical experience about the father's significance.

ORDER AND A GUIDING HAND

The father represents order and the establishment of a path of consciousness. Jim Fitzgerald, a Jungian analyst, writes about the father's shadow and the source of the masculine. Using the following ancient symbolism he depicts with great clarity, the father son relationship and the role of the father in the development of his son. 'On a stone pillar from Ancient Babylon, called the stele of Hammurabi and dating from about 2,000B.C., there is an image of the Sun-God Shamash presenting two objects to his earthly son, the King Hammurabi. These are a ring and a staff, the emblems of Kinship. They are to be found again in the sceptre and the orb used in coronation ceremonies, and in the ring and the crosier at the consecration of a bishop'.

Joseph Campbell, in *The Mythic Image*, interprets them as follows: the ring represents the full circle of the world's horizon, which the King as its pivotal staff is herewith ordained to establish and maintain in justice. Fitzgerald suggests that these are the symbols of the archetypal masculine, its earthly and heavenly, or static and dynamic aspects. The staff represents the centre that gives structure and order: the ring, the boundary that extends into the world and provides protection'[4]. This is symbolised by the circle and the staff. So that the father provides a container (the circle, the world) and the staff which represents the dynamic column extending out into the world on behalf of his child. He must establish a clearing, a path of consciousness. The father then has something to do with helping the child develop a perspective and establish a path of consciousness.

The father acts as a guide to his child. He helps him establish a sense of identity as separate from mother. He brings order to chaos. His guidance enables the child to emerge from the mass of undifferentiated earth matter from whence he was created. He helps the child begin to negotiate the world, to take his first halting steps away from mother and the safety of her womb. He enables the child to begin to form his own identity and consciousness. If this guidance is missing, then it will be more difficult for the child to fight his way out into consciousness. The result is confusion, disorder and a tendency to fall back into undifferentiation, or to regress back to the womb.

This happened to James quite a bit. James came to see me as a mature man, but his lack of fathering often made it feel as though I was working with a small confused boy. James lost his father just at the time when he would naturally have been in the process of breaking away from his mother. As a result, he often felt confused when called upon to be decisive or to take action. In the midst of what he saw as demands by others, and his partner Isabel in particular, he lost what decisive active male strength he had and he became lost in confusion. Losing his foothold, he floundered about in the sea of his conflicting feelings, unable to assert himself because he did know who he was or what he wanted. At such times, he lost his penetrative ability. To establish a path of consciousness for himself became a tremendous struggle. This is because in James the father was weak, tentative and easily toppled. By this I mean that James's inner father was not solid and well grounded. His outer father had been a distant somewhat forbidding figure and so the boy had difficulty reaching him. His lack of father made James lose confidence in himself. His self-esteem plummeted and he didn't trust himself. He didn't trust himself to be a man.

THE PUER

The father archetype has an inherent polarity. The structure-giving pole embodies the *Senex* or the 'old man' energy, which gives strength, order and endurance. At the other end of this is the *Puer* or eternal boy energy, which embodies freedom from restriction and the ability to break out of the mould. The more positive side of the missing father in the father/son psychological dynamic is the often strong constellation of the 'eternal boy' energy, which can be very creative because, like a child, it is innovative and likes to try new things. This imbues James and men like him with that endearing charming eternal youth energy that women find so attractive. It is a Peter Pan energy. It is a creative energy, which if harnessed positively enables the individual to transcend the usual boundaries of tradition and cultural mindsets and create something new. We need it in order to overcome obstacles to growth and evolution. We need it in order to grow and have the courage to change. It enabled me for example, to transcend and overcome the limitations of my own internal and external life and write this book.

Puer energy pushes the boundaries and brings about change. In Greek mythology the God Hermes symbolises this ability to move between two worlds. Hermes is a shape shifter, bringing about change through creating unrest or upheaval. Upsetting the natural order of things in order to bring about change is what he is all about. If we don't have an adequate amount of activated Hermes energy within us, we feel and remain stuck. Saturn represents the opposite to Hermes. He is the Father God and represents the old order. In the father/son dynamic, in order to develop a strong masculine, there needs to be a balance between both poles of this archetype, the Puer representing the son and the Senex the old man.

James had activated his Puer energy, but because he lacked the Senex quality, often he could not bring his creativity to ground; he could not harness it or actualise it. This left him 'up in the air' like the mythical figure Icarus who flew too close to the sun and then plummeted to earth and was lost. His fear of being 'defined' or grounded was given expression in his obsession with freedom, or what it was that he imagined freedom to be. James was afraid of being pinned down. Fearing failure in the face of life's struggles, he preferred to remain between the earth and the sky where he didn't have to account for himself, where he could drift along quite happily. His fear of getting 'stuck' by being given form meant that paradoxically, he was stuck. He was stuck because, like Icarus, he was so busy flying he didn't see the ground. He was out of touch with reality and so had great difficulty making his way in the world.

If the Puer energy is strong in a man and a strong internal father does not temper it, he often prefers to 'play'. So, he remains a boy at heart, a Peter Pan who does not want to grow up. He lacks guidance in how to negotiate the world and find a secure place in it. He is seeking a strong father to help him do this. The father's guidance is also necessary for his male child because the father is the archetype of male initiation. It is in his father that the male child will find the key to his own identity as a male. A boy's father is his role model. It is through identification with his father that the boy learns to negotiate the world and make the transition from boy to man.

PROTECTION AND BOUNDARIES

What else does the father bring to his child? He brings protection. One usually thinks of the mother as the person who provides protection for the child. But the father's protection is of a different quality. I once heard someone use the analogy of a bird's nest to describe the father's protective function. In the nest image we have the image of the double container, one inside the other. The outer layer is rough because it secures the nest to the tree or other object. It is on the outside. The outer layer also contains a dynamic conducting mechanism, creating order out of chaos, you could say. The inner layer of the nest is softer and contains the maternal matrix. This is like the mother. A child grows and develops in the womb and is protected there from the demands of being in the world. After birth the child still needs the protection of the mother while he or she gradually develops sufficient resources to stand alone. At that point the father comes in as a helper. He helps the child loosen his ties with the mother and begin to take his own steps in the world.

A good father relationship will help the child build up confidence in his own abilities. He needs this in order to feel strong enough to leave mother. At a very fundamental level, it is the masculine principle that helps us establish our boundaries in relation to the creative matrix. It is the animus/masculine principle that carries the feminine/receptive principle out into the world. And it is the marriage of both, which creates balance. From a psychological perspective the mother and the father function as inner principles, and what is always aimed for is the inner marriage. The inner marriage is the union of the masculine and the feminine principle within us, so that we find balance and harmony.

From the initial safety of the maternal container, the child begins to venture out into the outside world under the protection, as it were of the father. Psychoanalyst Peter Bloss suggests that the pre-oedipal father is a source of protection against the powers of regressive neediness, symbolised in this case by the mother. In other words the father helps the child negotiate the transition from the womb to the world, and he aids the child in separating from the mother. This is such an important and complex operation, with profound implications for the future life of the child that I will elaborate on it later on.

In the case of the son, the father activates sameness and gender identity. Jung writes that 'For the boy, the father is an anticipation of his own masculinity, conflicting with his wish to remain infantile' [5]. For both boys and girls, in this early stage the father helps the child build his or her boundaries by acting as a source of protection from the powers of regression to the collective level. He helps the child build a sense of him or herself as separate from mother and others. He is present at the awakening of ego consciousness. He helps the child have a sense of himself and say 'no' or 'yes' to both the outside world and his own inner world populated by instincts and desires.

THE PERSONA

The father helps us negotiate the world. In other words, he creates a safe place for the child in the world outside the one that he has previously inhabited with his mother. As the child begins to negotiate the outside world, he gradually builds up his *Persona*. The father is crucially important to the formation of the persona. This is a term used by Jung to describe the part of us that has acquired the social skills necessary to function effectively in the outside world. Jung takes Persona from the Greek word, which referred to the actor's mask worn in ancient ritual plays. This way, the Persona refers to the roles we play on the world stage. Its formation is the result of our innate drive towards adaptation to external reality and collectivity. It appears in dreams in the image of clothes, uniforms and masks. A person with an undeveloped or inadequately formed persona will dream of being at an elegant party dressed in rags, for example, or of being on stage and not knowing his lines, or his part.

It is very common, particularly during stressful times, to have dreams of failing exams or of not being adequately prepared for a task. Travelling and not having one's luggage is a common anxiety dream. Being on stage and not knowing one's part is a typical example. They all symbolise the fear of not having an adequate persona or the ability to successfully negotiate the world. These dreams often pass once the outside situation has been resolved.

In childhood our roles are set by parental expectations. The persona is built up gradually in the personality and is initially made up of the child's introjection of parental values. The first pattern of ego formation is to behave in such a way as to gain approval from the parents. The first persona therefore is made up of collective cultural codes of behaviour and value judgements as they are expressed and transmitted through the parents. A child will be brought up according to his parent's moral social and cultural values. But, in the course of normal psychological development, it is necessary for a differentiation between ego and persona to occur. This means the child needs to become aware of himself as an individual apart from the external 'collective' demands of society. He needs to become an individual with his own ideas and behavioural code. At the same time he has to live in the world and adapt to collective norms. In other words we need to learn to be ourselves but still occupy a professional or social position in relation to the world. So, we need to develop an adequate ego and an adequate persona. If this differentiation fails to occur, a pseudo-ego develops or is formed, and this means almost exclusive identification with one's role.

THE SHADOW

However, although it is important to have an adequately formed persona in order to function in the outside world, if the persona is too rigid or bright, then its opposite, the shadow will be all the darker for being repressed. The *Shadow* is a term Jung used to describe all that we are not consciously aware of. Often our more negative aspects, or the parts of our natures that we repress in order to please others, form part of our shadows. But the shadow can also contain our potentialities, things that we have not yet brought into life. The aim of Jungian analysis is to become individuated, which, in effect, is a coming into a sense of wholeness. In order to become whole, we must bring into awareness and integrate our shadows. It is the shadow that gives us depth, makes us more real. If we are all persona then we are not very genuine, for we are out of touch with our inner, real selves. Jung describes it thus: 'The man with the persona is blind to the existence of inner realities, just as the one lacking a persona is blind to the reality of the world. And 'it is better to take the line that the world is outside and inside, that reality falls to the share of both'⁶

STRUCTURE AND SPINE

The father also gives the child structure. He gives him backbone. Jungian analyst and author Guy Corneau and others, who have studied the psychological influence of fathers on their children and on sons in particular, suggest that unfathered sons are disorganised from within. They fear falling apart, or not having structure. We saw this with James, where he feared not being strong enough, particularly in the face of chaos or confusion. I have many other clinical examples of men burdened with this feeling. In all of them, what was needed and craved for was a connection with their father or the father energy, with their father's strength. Symbolically, the father represents the structure of the spine denoting support from the inside, from within. If a father is absent or negative, the son or daughter may not feel strong, and there will be a problem of boundaries.

The building of a personal sense of boundaries is a necessary part of personality development in both sons and daughters. If the father is absent the son may never develop the sense of having boundaries and being able to stand firm, and so he may have problems in intimate relationships with women. As a man he will fear loss of himself to a woman. He may, at a very unconscious and primitive level, fear engulfment by the feminine, and so will have a fear of intimacy, especially in sexual relating. At a fundamental level, I believe this represents fear of not feeling strong enough to separate from mother, and at a deeper level again, incorporation by the Great Mother. (I will deal with this in greater detail further on in the book).

The key point here is that the father brings strength and structure to a child and that being without this creates a fear of being overwhelmed by chaos or disorder. A sense of inner chaos will push the individual to compensate with compulsive behaviour and unnatural adherence to routine. The more compulsive a person is the greater is his or her fear of chaos. It is as if by building an external wall the person will manage to function and maintain an illusion of strength. But there will be little or no free flow of energy as it is unnatural to be so rigid. It is not healthy either.

It is interesting to compare father with the spine. The spine is central to the functioning of our bodies. If we suffer serious injuries to the spine we cannot function, we are without support. Symbolically, it is said that our spine represents our home base, our support system. Back problems suggest difficulties with supporting ourselves, with feeling supported. Like many others, I have suffered back pain during those times in my life when I have felt unsupported, or when I was unable to support myself. This is because father helps his daughter as well as his son to develop inner strength. A little girl who hasn't experienced the strong guidance of her father will find it harder to feel confident in negotiating her way in the world. Father helps us to develop self-confidence and an ability to fight for our needs and rights. If we perceive him as weak, then we may have difficulty asserting ourselves. As adult women we may then project this need onto the men in our lives.

SEPARATION FROM MOTHER

Helping the child to separate from mother is one of the father's singularly most important functions. In order to grow, the child must gradually loosen his or her ties with the mother. It is the father that helps us to do that. Freud and others emphasise the role of the father in allowing the separation process from the mother to begin. Psychoanalytic theorists such as Lacan[8] write in terms of Desire. The child will as a matter of course link itself with the mother's desire thereby guaranteeing immediate survival and complete dependence. In the ideal, the incoming child will be the desire of the parents. In a more embodied sense, the child is the object of the mother's desire.   However, I think that using the term desire can be misleading as the child can become lost in the mother's desire or need instead of existing for itself or it's own integrity. It is not uncommon for women to conceive babies to fulfil an objective of their own. Often this is done unconsciously, to mend a marriage or relationship, to 'keep' a lover, or sometimes even to fill an empty longing within. Burning with an inner emptiness, a woman imagines that if she had a child of her own, she would never be lonely again.

But, a child must ultimately grow beyond the mother's desire to find his or her own place in the world. It is the father who can guide the child to do this. He must at some level intervene in the mother/child relationship to allow the child gain access to his or her own originality, creativity and truth. The symbolic separation between the mother and the child is paramount to the psychological survival and development of the child.

The father represents the 'symbolic order', the order of culture, language and development. He represents the world of difference beyond the imaginary order. According to McKeown this can be seen as a three-stage separation process.[8]

'Firstly the mother's desire must be directed or focused outside herself: something other than the child must be in her life. As we have seen, this is to break a potential symbiotic and destructive dependency emerging between the mother and the child. Secondly, the father stands in the crucial position of this 'other', and he must be significant enough so as to capture the desire of the mother. The father must somehow represent the 'phallus'. Thirdly, the child follows the mother's desire outside herself, thus moving toward 'otherness'. It is crucial that the mother has desires outside herself. Thus the father must be 'present', at the very least metaphorically, so as to symbolically engage both the child's and the mother's desire'.

As the child begins the painful process of separation from his cosy and exclusive relationship with the mother, he turns to his father. In turning to the father, the child is also turning to the world of difference, the world of symbols and culture. According to McKeown, Lacan is not as naive as Freud in that he is quick to point out that the child soon discovers that the father is 'lacking' and does not have all the answers. Also his desire is focussed elsewhere. This too forms part of the process of separation and individuation for the child, and, painful as it may be, it initiates the child into a world of questioning and mystery outside itself. A world that is paradoxically frightening and wonderful. Ultimately and most importantly, it allows the child to begin the journey of discovering his or her own unique desire and place in the world.

BREAKING THE BOND

Jungian analyst and author Robert Bly writes very eloquently about how the father must intervene in the conspiracy between mother and son.[9] Most of us are familiar with this conspiracy. It is very strong in certain cultures. It is a strange sort of conspiracy, a type of bond that exists often unconsciously between mothers and their sons. Songs and folklore, which refer to this conspiracy, abound. It can be very strong and some men never break free of it. It is the cause of much heartache for those women in love with men who are still in the conspiracy, and who through their own love, seek to break the old outworn bonds that keep their lovers tied. 'Mother-bound' men are often attractive to women. They are also a terrible disappointment, for they are incapable of commitment. And if they do commit, they will often project all their unresolved childhood feelings onto their partners, turning their wives into their mothers. This is especially so when the son has a creative/artistic bent, and so a bond with mother is formed which excludes father. A very creative boy will be open to the energy of the feminine and therefore open to his mother in a very powerful way. If he does not feel or experience the energy of his father, he may remain enmeshed with the feminine in such a way as will make his life difficult. In order for the son to achieve his masculinity and 'become a man', this conspiracy must be broken. The bond with mother must be severed as the umbilical cord is severed at birth.

Bly describes it 'When the father lives his primary life away from the house, the mother often lacks a resonating box, if we might describe it so, where her longing for a close relationship with a man can resonate. She may then choose her son. When this happens, the son receives the intensity that should better be absorbed by a man the mother's own age, and this incoming intensity, using his body as a resonator, seems a burden to him as well as a secret pleasure. A sort of conspiracy develops, conducted in secret as true conspirators are, and the two conspirators-mother and son- push the father away still further.'

The son receives psychic heat, flattery, attention, support, and the feeling of being special for his part in this conspiracy; but he also becomes elevated to an adult, even Godlike status too early. As a result of being deemed a God he can lose contact with his father, and indeed the rest of the whole human world. He often grows into a man obsessed by his own image and importance, like Narcissus who fell in love with his own image and who drowned in it. This man becomes so blinded by his own image that he is incapable of loving another. He is in love with himself.

James was very indulged by his mother when he was a child. A charming sweet boy, he was sensitive and artistic. His mother idolised him, especially after the death of his father with whom she did not have a close relationship. When her husband died, she drew James closer to her with the invisible bonds of love and admiration as well as the desire to possess and control. She was proud of her handsome little son. She wanted to keep him with her. Sensing his unique position in his mother's life, he grew up consequently, with a great sense of his own importance. This surfaced most particularly in his relationships with women. As an adult man however, James' narcissistic streak was cleverly hidden under a veneer of charm and goodwill, which made him likeable and popular.

DIFFERENCE AND OTHERNESS

The father also represents difference and otherness. He helps the child move away from his or her primal state. The child knows its mother. It has grown inside her body and initially feels part of her. The father is someone 'different', not of mother. Therefore he is crucial to the child's sense of 'otherness' or difference. The presence of the father helps the child to establish a sense of his or her own individuality. It helps us to break out of the maternal shell from which we have emerged. He represents something and someone else and can begin to give us a sense of our own separateness. A weak or absent father can result in the fear of being trapped by the feminine and fear of intimacy in both men and women. It can make it hard for us to grow up, and so we remain infantile at heart. Without the strong father energy to help us separate, we remain caught in the maternal web. For the boy, a weak masculine will most certainly complicate his relationships with women, whom he may either consciously or unconsciously fear. Women will represent mother and if he is not strong in his masculine identity he will fear losing himself in love. For the girl, a weak masculine will mean she may remain incarcerated in the feminine shadow and lack individual boundaries. As a consequence, she will fear her own vulnerability and find it hard to 'hold her own' in the outside world and in relationships. As an adult woman she will undoubtedly project 'animus' or the inner masculine onto her partner and unconsciously expect him to provide boundaries for her.

Isabel was like this. She never really experienced her father as strong. Her childhood home was dominated by the overriding and unpredictable moods of her mother, which her father could not handle. He was a gentle natured man, who, like many men had great difficulty dealing with his feelings and relating emotionally. He was unavailable to her or to the rest of the family. He had taken refuge in the 'spirit', the imaginary world of thoughts and ideas. He was gifted with a great ability to write and talk about things on an intellectual level. On an emotional level, he had simply opted out. This meant that there was no protection from the manipulative ties and the web that Isabel's mother created and in which they were all imprisoned. Somewhere in her little girl's heart, Isabel missed him. Needing to break free from her complicated and overpowering mother, she missed the smell and feel of him. She missed the boundaries he could have erected around Isabel's mother to protect the little girl.

She grew up with a hunger and an emptiness, which she was quite unaware of consciously. In her relationships with men she looked for the missing essence of her father. She chose emotionally unavailable men of course; both her destiny and the unfinished business of her childhood pulled her there. Looking for strength and structure, she often chose men who could provide this for her in the material sense only. The relationships never worked. Her hunger remained. She did not know then that the strength she was seeking was inside her and only she could find it.

LANGUAGE

Most psychologists agree that the Father is important in the development of language in the child. Speech represents the ability to symbolise experience, as the child moves from bodily experiencing to being able to express itself verbally. Since archetypally the father represents tradition and collective consciousness, he establishes for the child, a link to the Divine Word. I imagine this means that it is through the father that the child connects with spirit. It is through this that the child connects to his own spirit. Spirit in this sense means the ability to think and to imagine, as well as to experience bodily sensations and instincts. In terms of child development, this also coincides with the anal phase and the beginnings of gender identity, which is a major transitional and maturational stage in the life of the child. The child gradually develops a sense of 'how to be' in the outside world, what is acceptable and not acceptable, as well as the gradual ability to symbolise experience. The father enables or creates a transitional space within which the child can begin to find or establish his identity. He establishes a clearing for the child so he can begin to see, feel, hear and regard himself as separate and individual. Becoming aware of 'spirit' and finding a connection with the Divine Word helps the incarnated soul to remember who he or she really is. Spirit in this sense has both an ordering capacity and a generative one, which has to do with knowledge.

Jung also suggests that the father represents clarity of insight and the ability to focus. My own interpretation of this is that it has something to do with the mind and the ability to be self-reflective. When we are too caught up in our emotions we cannot think straight. If on the other hand, we are connected to our feelings and able to enlist our mind, then we are in balance, we are acting with a sense of clarity and purpose. Often however, there is a confusion in us caused by our emotions, and so we lose our reflective ability. This is partly because with the general repression of feminine consciousness, we lose touch with our feelings and how to deal with them. All too easily they become a part of ourselves that we fear and mistrust. This body mind split causes many of us, and men in particular, to elevate logic and the ability to think in the abstract, at the expense of feelings and intuition which are regarded as inferior and therefore not to be trusted.

In essence, we are both and we need both. Jung used the term *animus* to describe the masculine aspect in women, the inner image of man. The animus like its counterpoint in men, the *anima*, is a soul image. It is an archetypal force and is not gender related in the sense that all men and women have masculine and feminine energies. Some Jungian writers have suggested that the animus in a woman represents her ability to be self-conscious, i.e. self-reflective. If as women we connect with a positive animus, then we are able to act with clarity and focus. We are able to use our minds to sort out our feelings and make sense of them. By that I don't mean getting rid of feelings, I mean understanding them and giving them meaning so that we can see things clearly. Like women, men need to have access to their ability to focus and see clearly in order to not become lost in their feelings. Clarity of insight comes from spirit.

SYMBOLS AND CULTURE

The father introduces the world of symbols and culture. He introduces consciousness. He is also the embodiment of the traditional spirit as expressed in religion or a general philosophy of life.[10] The father is the representative of the spirit, whose function is to oppose pure instinctuality. That is his archetypal role.[11] Jung considered that the resistance of the conscious mind to the unconscious and the depreciation of the latter were historical necessities in the development of the human psyche. Otherwise the conscious mind would never have been able to differentiate itself at all. This has its corollary in the mother and child separation phenomenon I wrote about earlier. A child has to separate out in order to 'grow' into himself. He does this by gradually building up an individual ego and separate consciousness.

In Jung's view modern man's consciousness has strayed rather too far from the unconscious, a view with which I concur. This has to do with a splitting, whereby mind and matter are separated and one (mind) becomes elevated above the other (matter). Worse, the mind becomes associated exclusively with the masculine while matter becomes synonymous with the feminine. This creates all sorts of difficulties, of which our modern 'loss of soul' is just one example. It creates a world of separation, a split world where patriarchal structure involves the cutting off of feeling or feminine consciousness. This does not serve modern man well since a divorce from nature means the death of the soul at some deep level. A soul does not like to be split and this can be observed in the quest for wholeness amongst individuals today.

FAMILY LEGACY

A father will pass on his legacy to his son and to his daughter. This is often observed in families where traditionally it is the son who becomes 'heir'. The father often unconsciously brings to his son all of his own father's legacy, whether expressed through the entitlement to family property and estate or inheritance, or through feelings and thoughts. If a father has been disinherited, say, this fact and feelings of emasculation, betrayal or sense of injustice will often pass to his son and would be 'heir'. If the father has internalised a great sense of injustice then this will burn in his soul and his son will sense it and sometimes may continue to carry the torch for his father.

Take the story of John who could not inherit because he was the second son of a traditional family where the eldest son was deemed heir. Growing up, nothing much was expected of him. His brother, by contrast, was treated very much as the heir, and serious thought was given to his development and education. John reacted to this by becoming the clown and amusing everyone. He was blessed with a naturally sunny personality, which he cultivated in order to please people and gain their approval. He was allowed to grow up without much guidance, and since nothing much was expected from him, no one took him very seriously. Deprived of his 'legacy' or birthright in some way, he felt profoundly disempowered. Beneath his careful 'bright' and pleasant veneer he was seething with rage. Deep down he felt 'rubbished', not important. As a consequence he was prone to behaving irresponsibly as though defying a ghost father and seeking to be restricted or admonished. Not being aware, he never dealt with these feelings and they lay inside him like embers waiting to burst into flame.

When he got married, as luck would have it he also had two sons. To his eldest he passed on the legacy of 'son and heir' and treated him as such. His younger son Joe then found himself in the same position his father had been in. Clearly and painfully aware of his father's special bond with his older brother, Joe sought to please him. He craved his father's attention, and his special sensitivity and gentle nature meant that he often felt hurt and betrayed by his father's lack of awareness of him. But John was a remote type of parent who found it hard to relate to anyone intimately, and so their relationship acquired a formality that left Joe disappointed. Acutely and painfully aware of his father's wounds, Joe expressed his own father hunger by seeking to heal him. Somewhere he sought to empower his father. When he became an adult he tried to help him become aware and responsible. In short, Joe became father to his father.

We all want strong fathers. If we don't have them we compensate in one way or another. A boy like Joe will have found 'father' in other ways, from his mother's animus for example. But I believe his need to heal his father and empower him dates back to his own father's childhood and maybe even further beyond that. Our family legacy is determined for us before we are born. We 'inherit' thoughts, ideas, images and imprints from our parents. Some of these legacies span centuries. They are grafted into our psyches and are activated as we experience life. It is said that patriarchy is in our bones. We cannot escape our destiny but we can shape it.

DISCIPLINE: CLAIMING OUR SWORD

Jung also suggests that the father represents the world of moral commandments and prohibitions. This notion has its modern expression I think in that it is the father in a family who is generally invested with authority. It is he, usually the more remote of the parental pair whom the children are induced to obey. 'Wait till your father gets home!' are words we have all heard. Traditionally, we expect the father to be the one to discipline the children. This expectation I imagine, may well be part of how the father archetype is primed within us. Like the feeling of warmth and connectedness associated with mother, it is part of our ancient psyches. This authoritarian image is given modern expression in films, plays, dreams, myths, songs and stories, all of which inform us. In mythology it is generally the father Gods who are authoritarian and punitive and whose commands are obeyed or disobeyed.

Most if not all children will push the boundaries imposed on them by their parents by disobeying or being naughty. This impulse is part of growing up. As the child develops and grows, he forms an individual ego. He does this by pushing against and sometimes opposing parental values. In this way, the child grows into a state of individual consciousness and separates from his parents. The need to fight against the prevailing order is a necessary part of evolution and growth. In terms of the father son encounter this has a special flavour and energy. All sons have a need to 'surpass' their father in some way. Whether beating them at chess, going to university, getting a better job, or achieving through extending and developing their fathers' work, sons need to somehow surpass their fathers in order to become secure adult men and fathers. This again is an inner usually unconscious urging which gnaws at the young boy's soul and spurs him into maturity. In order to understand the 'inside story' of men, both in relation to women and as fathers, we need to look in more detail at the father/son relationship.

Notes

1.   D. Kay, In *The Father*, edited by Samuels, A. Free Association Books (1985) p.45
2.   C.G. Jung, *The significence of the father in the destiny of the individual*. CW4 paras 301-323
3.   Ibid., para 728
4.   J. Fitzgerald, *The father's shadow and the source of the masculine* (unpub lished work)
5.   Ibid., para 737
6.   Ibid., CW7 para 319
7.   in Changing Fathers, Ferguson, McKeown and Rooney, (1998) p.61
8.   Ibid., p.64
9.   in Mother/Father edited by Wilmer, H. Chiron (1990) p.8
10.   C.G. Jung, CW12 para 60
11.   ibid., CW 3 para369

CHAPTER FIVE

FATHERS AND SONS

There is a mysterious occurrence when the child is born. It's stunning to the son to realise that his father doesn't feel the delicate uncertainty with which he walks into life. The father and son are both shocked by the great longing they feel for each other and the way that they clash when they come close to one another. Between fathers and sons, a long distance grows easily, silences spread from something small to something wide and seemingly unending. Something mysterious connects them and something awkward and painful drives them apart'.

(Meade, M. Men and the Water of Life)

To the boy, his father is of major importance. It is he more than anyone who influences how this boy grows up to be a man. It is through his father that the boy gains access to his maleness. The boy will look at this father to see himself as a man. Many young boys say they want to be like Daddy when they grow up. This is natural and good. The father's presence influences and shapes the growing boy in a particular way. For him, his father is the anticipation of his own masculinity. It is from his father that he gets the raw materials that will activate his archetypal heritage; the programme in him called 'how to be a man'. A boy needs his father to activate his innate and prospective masculinity. In the absence of his father he will feel a gap. As Bly writes, when a boy does not see his father working for example, he will have to imagine him doing so, and a void will be created as a result. What does father do, and how does he do it? In time, if the presence of his father does not flesh out his imagination with real experience, then it may be filled by demons. The boy will have to find his own way to manhood without the guidance and role model of his father.

FATHER HUNGER

'Father hunger' is endemic in Western culture. As already stated, the Inner King is damaged. The Inner King is our image of father and all that he stands for. If he is wounded then he will be a Fallen King. Our Inner King is based on our perception and experience of our own father, and further back on the mythic images of fatherhood, as it comes down to us from the collective and our ancestors. Kings have died in the Western psyche because our more recent experience of fathers and fathering is that he is absent or ineffectual. Often taken captive by the feminine, this means we have inherited a weaker, less powerful image of the masculine. In actual physical terms father may not be absent but in some way his energy is weakened, and so he appears remote and isolated. Current social trends have ensured that this is often the case. He remains someone we seek a closer connection to. Although we look up to him, we often fear him and seek to please him. Closeness is not something we can count on with father and so he appears a more distant and less defined figure than mother.

In Western culture moreover, there has been a shaking up of the old order. Institutions such as the Church, political dictatorships, and traditional social system all are being questioned. The old vestiges of patriarchy are no longer serving our needs, and so we are forced to seek answers elsewhere. Our father hunger has made us question and seek answers in ourselves. This is perhaps a positive side effect of our insecurity. In the absence of an institutional, religious, political or social father who would support us and tell us how to live our lives, we have had to turn to our own selves. Ultimately we have to find and harness our own inner father.

DRAWING THE
MALE SOUL INTO THE WORLD

Both in personal terms and in terms of the father/son relationship this father hunger has many implications. A child needs a guide to help him develop as an adult. If his father is absent, the boy will take his role model from not only the male figures around him but from the dim memories of his grandfather or great-grandfather. He will probably not be able to recall these last two but in the rawness and emptiness that the absence of his father creates in his soul, the boy will cling to these memories and draw them closer to his bones. In the absence of a father, and anxious to give flesh to his maleness, the boy pulls on the archetypal image of the father to gain access to his own innate masculinity. Lacking the strength and security that connection with his real father could give him, the young boy's soul will develop a deep hunger and he will search for a male figure to fill the gap his lost father has created.

When a boy loses or does not know his father, the longing of it burns in his soul with a relentless ache. At such times he will try and draw closer to him undefined images of heroes to clothe his bones and draw his male soul into the world. When there is a father gap, it will be filled by other things that will leave an imprint on his psyche. His mother's inner male image, her animus, will fill the space, as will discarnate images of manhood from his dreams and fantasies. His inner world will be filled with heroes, warriors, soldiers and sages that his imagination will loosen at night to fill his dreams. The more remote or absent his connection with his personal father, the more the boy will be influenced by the archetypal father and the more difficult it will be for him to humanise the archetype and incarnate his male soul. In other words, the harder it will be for him to become a man and take his place in the world.

James lost his father when he was still a boy. He stills feels the gap left by his father at a time when he would naturally be drawing closer to him and pulling away from his mother. Although approaching middle age now, at a very fundamental level, he is unsure of himself as a man. In order to become a man this fatherless little boy had to draw on the archetypal father and on his family, societal and cultural heritage. In the absence of his father who would have rooted his maleness in embodied experience, he had to make do with something dimmer, less real. The father archetype was not humanised for him by his father. As a result James is very susceptible to what other people might think of him. He is very susceptible to behaving as society dictates a man should be, rather than who he really is. Not quite secure within himself, he unconsciously looks to other people for clues on how to be. He aims to please people. In Jungian terms, he is over identified with the persona, with his role in society and the part he is expected to play on the world stage.

IN THE NAME OF THE FATHER

How the son experiences and develops out of the father/son encounter and how the masculine archetype becomes incarnated in his psyche, are crucial for his life and destiny. The father/son archetype is the archetype of masculine initiation. As such it constellates at all transitional stages in a man's life, especially major ones such as when he goes to college, leaves home, procures his first job, gets married, and becomes a father. During all transitional stages there is a decentring, a loss of orientation. This is normal. When we are moving from one stage to another, we lose the ground that we were previously standing on. We often lose our way. Through connecting with the father/son archetype, meaning and order are restored. If the inner father is weak then all transitions will be experienced as difficult. A father hungry man will find it hard to set himself goals and will tend to be disorganised. Not having the required clarity and focus he needs to act with purpose and definition, he may be inclined to drift. He may also allow situations to drift. He will be more likely to be reactive rather than proactive.

According to Jungian analyst Jim Fitzgerald, recent studies have noted that, for the boy, 'the father becomes a focus of attention quite separate from the mother at a much earlier point than the Oedipal stage, which is where Freud placed the emphasis.' To quote American psychoanalyst Peter Bloss, ' The pre-oedipal father provides the boy with a source of security and the implicit protection against the powers of regressive neediness; in addition, the pre-oedipal father activates in the little boy the experience of male congruity and sameness. Partaking in the father's maleness represents the early stage of gender identity'.[1] Bloss suggests that if there is a failure in this early 'dyadic stage' of the father/son relationship 'the life of the adult male will encompass an unceasing search for father imagos and the son will be left with a lifelong father-hunger'.

Many psychologists suggest that the time of emancipation from mother is the most formative period of the boy's life. It is the period when the boy child moves from continuity with and dependence on mother to focus on the father. This transitional stage has to do with the crystallisation of the masculine ego out from the maternal containment. It is a crucial time for the boy. The manner in which the father 'complex' becomes established in the son's psyche, and the manner in which it constellates, decides the course and destiny of his life. Its constellation will depend on the way in which the personal father mediates the archetype for his son. The father archetype is triggered into action by the son's encounter with the personal father, at this transitional time when there is a 'readiness' in the son's psyche. The boy will actively seek it out and be ready for it. Through identification with a 'loving' father, he is implanted with the seed of his future masculinity.

He is also given a sense of continuity with his line of male ancestors, which mediates the primordial masculine essence. This is important for the boy, as it enables him to have access to the creative spirit of the unconscious in a full way. He will have a sense of history, of what the men in his family were like, a sense of their taste and their smell. He will have a feeling sense of what being a male in the context of his larger 'family' is all about. He will receive the legacy of his father, grandfather and male ancestors. This information may not be fully conscious, but it will inform his psyche and influence his transition from boy to man. Soldiers, scholars, poets, workers and players, they will all be there. They will dance in and out of his dreams. His father brings him these memories by his very presence. Every boy, and every girl, is influenced by the mythic images of male and female as handed down by generations of family.

IN HIS FATHERS HOUSE

The father provides his son with strength and structure. Corneau writes: 'An individual's psychological identity is based on his sense of his own spine, which provides him with support from the inside. The father's absence results in the child's lack of internal structure: this is the very essence of a negative father complex. An individual with a negative father complex does not feel himself structured from within'[2]. Fatherless boys are usually short on guidance and long on desire. When a boy lacks a father he loses out on the guidance needed to help him build a solid spine, a solid base, and a sense of himself as strong. This usually means he will look for it in others. But, lacking the emotional and mental vocabulary to deal with it, he may also resent it. He may become rebellious in an unconscious attempt to find 'father'. Or he may develop a rigid persona and obsessive-compulsive behaviour as a way to keep himself 'in order'. Lacking inner strength he erects rigid outer structures to stop himself falling apart.

As we saw in the chapter about the father's birth gifts, he provides protection and as well as boundaries. Fitzgerald writes 'The father provides boundaries in two ways: he protects the boy from the intrusions of the outer world, and enables him to build up a satisfactory persona. He also provides limits to the instincts and drives which might invade from the unconscious'. This is a very important point and one which Jung himself addressed in his own paper 'Anima /Animus'.[3] 'Just as the father acts as a protection against the dangers of the external world and thus serves his son as a model persona, so the mother protects him against the dangers that threaten from the darkness of his psyche. In the puberty rites, therefore, the initiate receives instruction about these things of 'the other side' so that he is put in a position to dispense with his mother's protection.'

Jung is referring to the father's role as guide or helper in negotiating the outside world. He also points to the fact that it is important that the son move from his mother's to his father's protection. In so doing, the boy will be forming his own anima or inner image of woman and this will be very much based on his experience of his mother. But in order to progress into manhood he must leave his mother's house and join his father's. This is the very essence of male initiation. As Jung points out, modern civilised man has had to forgo this primitive system of education. Modern man has no system of initiation comparable to the initiation rites of traditional cultures. This makes the transition from boy to man more difficult. Because the initial breaking away has not happened, the 'anima' projection is transferred to his wife, lover or the woman in his life.

REMAINING IN HIS MOTHER'S HOUSE

What happens when father is absent or has not intervened to help the boy separate from his mother? When a man remains identified with his mother he remains fused with his unconscious; he is his own desires, his impulses, his ideas. He has no access to his own individuality and the fact that he does not have to obey the dictates of both his internal and external world. In other words it is hard for him to know what he wants and to measure his needs and responsibilities so that he can live a balanced life. You could say that he has not differentiated himself enough to form a strong, separate individual ego. And so he is not strong, although he may appear so on the outside. Unconsciously, he seeks structure. But because it is an unconscious need, he also fears and resents it. James and other men like him, tend to attract strong women on whom they then project 'animus' or father. They are attracted to strong women because they seek strength in themselves. Lacking a decisive, active, penetrating energy, they leave decisions and action to their women and then often complain about 'being controlled'.

Isabel wondered why James had trouble making decisions. She also feared making them herself because she did not want to be accused of being controlling. And so in their relating things were often allowed to drift. She wanted him to 'be a man' and do the 'manly' things, not because she was not 'liberated' but because deep in her heart she wanted her man to be the strong one. She wanted to be able to lean on him, to hug his hard protective frame when she needed security. Deep down he wished to protect her too. But somewhere the wires got tangled and it all went wrong. His thoughts were confused, and this made it difficult for him to make decisive decisions. Being a decisive person herself, she would become fed up with the airiness of his ways. And he would pull away from her, fearful of being sucked into something although he didn't know what. Because James's inner father was weak, at a very deep level he felt unable at times to stand up to his inner mother and therefore to Isabel. And because Isabel, although strong, had a father hunger too, she wanted James to be her strong decisive King. When he didn't deliver, she was bitterly disappointed. James intuitively knew this. He was keenly aware of her disappointment in him and this only exacerbated his hidden but very real sense of inadequacy.

Lacking a father therefore is like not having a spine. People often refer to people whom they consider weak as 'spineless'. There is nothing worse for any man either young or old than to be considered spineless. It will hurt a father hungry man most, for that is what he fears most. The unfathered man will have trouble setting himself goals, making choices, deciding what's good for him and identifying his own needs. Seeking structure, yet resenting it, he will often project it onto others, thereby complicating his relationships. Many unfathered men will over compensate as James does, by structuring themselves from the outside.

'SEARCH FOR THE HERO INSIDE YOURSELF'

When a man considers himself unstructured internally, he compensates by trying to build an external structure. This is when the Hero is born. Carrying a fragile internal masculine identity, the Hero builds an outer shell to hide his vulnerability. The Hero archetype constellates strongly in the boy who has an absent father but very present and strong mother, because she will project her animus onto him along with all her unfulfilled dreams. And so we get phrases like 'my son the priest', 'my son the doctor', and so on. A mother who brings up her son or sons alone will be particularly prone to project her animus ideals along with her unfulfilled ambitions onto them.

When the Hero archetype constellates strongly in a boy, he will over identify with the persona at the expense of his own inner life. It is easy to recognise the Hero type. He belongs to society and has never been born to himself. He may cry out 'let me be myself' to the women in his life, but he is always drawn to what he believes others want him to be, or more accurately, what he thinks a man ought to be. The latter will of course be dictated by what is culturally acceptable as male attitudes and behaviours. And since the Hero often lacks a father and is therefore mother-bound, an internal judging mother whom he does not have the strength to resist judges all his actions. Such a man is very sensitive to criticism, his own internal critic most of all. He always seeks to shine, to achieve. He overworks and rarely allows himself to really relax. He is overly critical and never happy with what he has achieved. Therapists' consulting rooms are filled with people who regard themselves as failures.

Corneau uses the Greek myth of *Icarus* to illustrate this over identification with the need to shine, to achieve, and to seek external recognition and approval. *Icarus*, the son of *Horus*, flew too close to the sun and was destroyed by it. His waxen wings began to melt as he flew higher and higher and closer to the sun, and he plummeted into the sea. Drawn by the brightness of the sun and intoxicated with the freedom of flying, he had ignored the advice of his father to fly neither too high nor too low. And so he fell to the sea and drowned. This is where we are doomed to go when we overdo it. Seeking perfection, we experience burnout. As Jung puts it 'The sacrifice that signals the individual's separation from his mother also signals a renunciation of his own importance'.[4]

What the Hero needs most is to become more real to himself. He needs to be less identified with the role of the hero, and instead to find the hero within himself. Becoming aware that he has sacrificed his inner light for outer recognition will be a necessary part of finding the hero within. This means looking inwards, something many men find difficult. Having identified with what the prevailing culture expects a man to be, the hero has great difficulty believing that there is anything to be gained from looking inside himself. Focused on achieving in the 'outer world', he does not believe there is anything of value in his inner world. Nonetheless, he must do this if he is to find the hero inside himself.

Getting in touch with his feelings can help him to reconnect with his true nature. Feelings are our roots in life and once we lose touch with them we experience 'loss of soul' and we too are lost. Our feelings and getting in touch with our inner selves actually connects us to others and ultimately to humanity. In psychological terms this means allowing our shadow to come through. It is our shadow that gives us depth and helps us to see that everything isn't black and white or one-dimensional. Acknowledging our feelings helps us evaluate ourselves when we might otherwise be lost in the sea of others' and our own desires. Facing our fears and acknowledging our humanity connects us to all of life and ultimately with God. It makes us real. We fly then neither too low nor to high. We are balanced.

James was a Hero. Inside his hero's costume and soldier's armour, he had a sweet soul and a gentle nature. His heart was filled with the capability to love; he was a lover at heart. Isabel knew this because she saw it in him. But James ignored it in himself. His gentle nature was a nuisance. His feelings were a nuisance. Not trusting himself or his loving nature, he sought always to achieve, to work, to shine. He was never good enough; he didn't work hard enough; he was lazy and indulgent. Part of him wished he did not possess a heart and feelings, because from past experience, he knew it only led him into pain and betrayal.

So Isabel was caught in a trap. She loved him and wanted him to be who he really was. She wished he could have opened his heart and beamed the sunshine she sometimes felt from him, onto her. At such times she turned towards him like a flower turns towards the sun. But if she voiced a need for him, he perceived it as an inadequacy within himself and retreated into his shell. He always imagined she was not 'pleased' with him. Isabel wondered whether at heart he never really felt good enough. She wondered whether at some level his mother was disappointed in him when he was a boy.

James too wanted Isabel. The only problem was she gave so easily he did not have to ask. She did not challenge him enough, and yet in a strange way, she challenged him more than he had previously been challenged in a relationship. Like many hurt men who have closed the doors of their hearts, he had lost touch with his own needs. Getting involved with Isabel meant relating more intimately than he had ever done before and it led him back to his own feelings. Over time, and as the relationship progressed, he gradually got in touch with his need for love, his need for her. He was afraid however that if he were to allow that awareness to become rooted in him, longing might flood his heart and he would not be able to bear the pain if he were to lose her. He had lost so many times before. James' previous unmourned losses, starting with his father, had built up a wall around his heart. He never allowed himself to really imagine he could be allowed to love and be loved in return. Love was a no go area for James.

SELF ESTEEM AND CONFIDENCE

A good relationship with father will heighten a boy's self-esteem. Research shows that a warm, affectionate relationship between father and son results in a strong development of male identity[5]. Some studies show that poorly fathered boys tend to be lacking in self-esteem or unsteady in their self-belief. This is perhaps because lacking a positive male role model they often repress their aggression and their ambitious natures.[6] Children who have been adequately fathered generally exhibit more self-confidence and personal initiative. I wonder if this is because a father's love tends to be expressed more conditionally; for example "If you succeed in x I'll give you y' as a way of encouraging the child's achievements. Mother's love is often expressed less conditionally outwardly at least, although in my view it can be just as conditional, just expressed differently. However, it is often the father who encourages the child to achieve.

I remember wanting to work hard to achieve good results at school really in order to please my father who always showed an interest in my academic ability and intellectual pursuits. Likewise, in my clinical practice, it is a common occurrence for men in particular to deplore the lack of interest their fathers took in their studies or achievements. I recall one man who described how he felt when, during a therapy session he had overhead my son speaking on the phone recounting his school examination results. He became quiet and sad, and told me that he'd wished someone had cared about his own exam results.

Some psychologists suggest that a father expressing love

conditionally encourages a boy's sense of responsibility. However, if the father pushes his son to achieve, and this is done without the love and warmth that he also needs, then it can have a negative rather than a positive effect.

Joe's father wanted his son to get a job during the school holidays. In itself this wasn't a bad thing, but at the age of fourteen, when most children were free to play and enjoy themselves, Joe felt it was an imposition and he resented it. Tired after the school year, he was never allowed a morning lie in during the holidays. His father John would 'hassle him' to get up. He himself had been brought up with a particularly strong work ethic, and so he knew no better. Unfortunately, he had projected his own fears of not being good enough and of being idle onto his son. Imbued with a great need to achieve in order to please his own father and mother, John thought he was doing the best for his son by pushing him. However, he was out of touch with his real needs. He was also out of touch with his son's needs, which were to be loved and accepted without having to produce or achieve.

CHANNELLING AGGRESSION

As I have already said, it is very common for little boys to want to grow up to be like daddy. Most psychologists agree that this is a positive and normal feature of growing up for boys. Boys seek a role model in their father, and if they don't find it in him they will generally project that need onto some other male figure. A love affair needs to take place between a father and his son. A very different type of love than that which exists between a son and his mother. A boy will look up to his father and seek to emulate him. In return the father guides the son in finding a purposeful goal or outlet for his natural aggression.

However, if the father is absent, weak, or perceived as emasculated by his children, then this comes as a terrible blow to his son. He may grow up despising his father's weakness and at the same time he may be acutely aware of his father's vulnerabilities and seek to protect him. A knot forms in the boy's chest, a knot of conflicting feelings of love and hatred, fear and anger. He may seek to protect his father from attack and yet at the same time he may be very angry that he himself is being deprived of a strong father. He may despise his father's weakness and feel his humiliation at the same time. In seeking a strong father in order to grow strong himself, he is unconsciously seeking to empower his father and consequently himself.

Peter felt this. His father was a gentle natured man who had been completely dominated by his wife. She made no secret of the fact that she had wanted daughters, and she treated her boys with the delicacy that would normally be reserved for girls. She would not allow any rough play, and by virtue of her repressed anger and by keeping her husband away from his sons, she managed to suppress their natural aggression. Because he never spent time with his sons, their mother claimed them. Anxious for peace at all costs, Peter's father retreated into himself and lost his spirit. No match for the strong and controlling woman he had married, he cowered under her whip, and by doing so, he failed his boys.

Peter remembers desperately wanting his father to be strong and to stand up to his mother. He hated the way his mother constantly put his father down. In a strange confusion of emotions, he felt tied to his mother through his anger and tied to his father because he wanted to protect him. Yet at the same time there was a dim awareness in him of the betrayal that he felt at the hands of his father. During our sessions, he found himself incessantly angry and frustrated. He felt disempowered; that he was only operating on three cylinders, not quite up to speed. Like a rusty engine, he merely limped through life. He had lost his spirit, his driving force, and his zest for life. When I asked him to describe this feeling, he said it felt as if there was a mattress pressing down on him. He associated this feeling with his mother.

When I brought up the subject of his father, Peter became emotional. In touch with his father's gentleness of spirit and his tender heart, Peter recalled his father with love. It appeared that it was through his father that Peter had learnt about love and tenderness. Even though they had not had an emotionally close relationship, Peter's boy soul longed for it. He craved more closeness yet he couldn't reach him. As a result of our working together, Peter became aware that he couldn't reach his own soul and his innate ability to love, because it was blocked by the anger and resentment he felt about his childhood. He was still carrying his father's repressed anger. His father was a wounded man, and Peter was wounded in that he had lost touch with his anima, his feminine side. He was also disempowered as a male. Since Peter's mother had totally repressed all his natural male aggression, and since his father was emasculated, Peter had very little to call on in terms of guidance on how to be a strong male.

How a boy perceives his father is extremely important and will influence him in his own growth to manhood. A boy may react to his father's emasculation at the hands of his mother by becoming domineering himself. He may be drawn to marry a woman whom he feels he can dominate and put down. He may become a controller and a bully as compensation for his feelings of inner powerlessness. Or he may do the opposite. He may marry a woman who will dominate and control him. An inner feeling of powerlessness may result in any one of a number of outcomes. The key point is that the mother/father relationship dynamic creates an energy that permeates all children. In particular it affects the way a son relates to his father and by definition, himself.

THE SHADOW OF THE FATHER

'What was silent in the father speaks in the son,
And often I found the son the unveiled secret of the father'

(Nietzsche, Thus Spake Zarathustra)

Nietzsche, I believe, speaks of the father's shadowy energy given expression in the life of his son. The son will carry certain aspects of his father's shadow and will quite unconsciously find himself living them. For it is an unwritten law that children live out their parents' unlived lives. James for example, wrote the books his father failed to write. And Isabel, she carried some of her mother's unlived dreams in her body, gave birth to them as children and later in her poetry. James's father died a relatively young man and so consequently it was easy to see that James was giving life to his father's dream.

Even if the father lives but remains unconscious and represses much of his own creativity, his son will often breathe

life into what remains hidden in the father. Such is the influence of the father archetype on a man. It is common for sons
to follow in their father's footsteps. If there are two or more
sons, then at least one will appear to take on the mantle of
their father. Sometimes a son will live out something of his
father's dream. For example, a father may have had a lifelong
dream of achieving fame as a musician. Preoccupied with the
tasks and responsibilities of marriage and becoming a parent,
he will have abandoned his boyhood dream. One of his sons
may later give life to this dream by becoming or tying to
become a musician.

What is unconscious forms the shadow. What the father
is not aware of in himself, and does not express or activate in
his life, will pass to his son in some shape or form. As I have
already said, it is the fate of all children to carry and in some
cases live out their parents' unlived lives. This is a very subtle
and complex process because it is what is unconscious in the
parent that is passed on. As Jungian analyst Von Franz puts it:
'When parents fail to live out their inner wholeness and fail to
realise substantial components of themselves, the weight of
these parts falls onto the children in the form of a projection
and endangers them. The children find themselves driven by
a dark compulsion to live out everything the parents have
repressed[7]'.

In the course of psychotherapy one aims to become conscious of the unconscious because we know that, ultimately,
what is unconscious kills you. By this I mean that what we are
unaware of in ourselves seeks to be known and so has a way
of intruding into our consciousness and our life one way or
another. The soul seeks wholeness. It does not like to be split.
If we continually repress and suppress what seeks to be
realised in us, we can eventually become ill. What we repress
or have not yet activated forms our shadow. When we recover our shadow we have a chance to become whole.

In terms of the father/son relationship this means that
the little boy will inherit all sorts of ideas, images, expectations and feelings from his father's shadow, all of which will
shape him during his transition to adulthood. These images
will guide him to behave in certain ways, and will prompt him
unconsciously to seek certain experiences and certain relationships. These inherited psychic imprints will also lend a particular flavour to how he relates to others.

MEN TO BE

How the father mediates the father archetype for his son is crucial. If the father archetype is evoked in its positive boundary-protecting qualities, then the transition is made to the next stage of life. Should these qualities be absent, and the transition not made, then the separation from the mother may not be effected and the son may remain unconsciously bound to her. In this case his masculinity remains liminal or latent. He remains stuck in the doorway to life, with no clearly defined masculine identity. He is then in effect a 'man to be', a liminal man, a man still in the process of becoming a man. There is a father hunger in the soul of the boy, and the unceasing search for the father imago (finding the male that will trigger the archetype in the psyche) will be awakened and released. When there is failure at this developmental stage, the bipolar masculine archetype does not become properly incarnated in the life of the son. The missing pole recedes into the unconscious, thereby becoming the core of the negative father complex. It exercises great power over the life of the son.

When there is failure to incarnate the wholeness of the archetype, one aspect remains in the shadow. As compensation, the masculine persona of the father is usually all the more inflated. This leads to an overdeveloped persona. The man becomes identified with 'what a man should be' rather than who he actually is. As Jung says, 'fundamentally the persona is nothing real: it is a compromise between the individual and society as to what a man should appear to be'. If the father's persona is divorced from the instinctual, physical and emotional aspects of masculinity these sink deeper into the unconscious and activate the archaic layers of the psyche. Father then becomes associated with spirit, the Sky God; something cut off from the earth and all things sensual. The king, who is the son of the Sky God, will always identify with the light. He will be suspicious of and shun the darker depths of his nature. Such a man will live totally in his head. To live elsewhere is dangerous.

The soul however, does not obey the dictates of any thought process. It simply is. Imagination is the language of the soul. Many of us are out of touch with our feelings and our intuition as a result of this body/mind division. We consider imagination to be at best, unreliable, at worst, worthless and a waste of our time. In general women tend to embody the 'feeling' part of the split. We can see evidence of this in the way society by and large teaches men to 'think and do' rather than 'feel and be', and so a man will often seek the solution to his psychological problems outside of himself rather than paying attention to his inner self.

OUTSIDE IN

Many men view things from the outside in rather than from the inside out. I often experience this in my consulting room. Women are much more likely to seek help in dealing with their inner feelings. They arrive knowing that any change has to come from the inside. Men by contrast, are likely to bring themselves to the consulting room rather as they would bring their car to the garage and ask for it to be fixed. I, the therapist, am supposed to become the mechanic who will tinker with their head as if it were the engine of a car, and thereby sort them out. In my experience, men often take longer to work through inner conflicts in therapy because they tend to hand over responsibility to me. They imagine that I can sort them out. They hand me the complicated bundle of their life problems and their dreams expecting me to return it to them repaired. Like some witch doctor, I am supposed to sort through the bones of their complicated inner lives and return it to them healed of pain. They imagine that I will cure them of their afflictions by surgically removing the poisonous illusions that have swelled their lives to an unbearable degree. At best, they imagine I can wave a magic wand and say 'all gone nasty Mummy and Daddy; all gone horrible feelings!'

This phenomenon is not of course exclusive to men! I think there is a small, unevolved part in all of us that desires a quick fix to pain. That being said, it often takes a great deal of time and patience for a hurt man to finally understand that he lives inside himself and that he is his own healer. And that although I am a therapist and therefore may have better spectacle lenses with which to see clearly in the dark, I am merely a benign presence, a fellow traveller. For a short time we will travel along the same road together.

Of course the vast majority of hurt men do not venture into therapy. Imbued with those elements of a cultural climate that make it hard for them to admit they need help, it is usually the women in their lives who brings them to counselling or therapy. In relationships, it is common for the woman to carry a lot of the feelings for both partners. Similarly, some men will overly depend on the women in their lives to act out their emotional side. This being so, it is through these women that so much is learnt about men, about their strengths and their vulnerabilities, about their fears and their loneliness. Women speak on behalf of men sometimes because, often lacking the emotional vocabulary which would enable them to speak for themselves, it can be the only way these men can be heard. I have no doubt that my consulting room will continue to be filled with the unspoken voices of such men. When men have regained what they have lost, they too will find their voices.

If the father has not passed on to his son the ability to be in touch with and to articulate his feelings, then this aspect of his personality will remain in the shadow. If the father has not integrated the shadow elements into his life, these are projected on to the son. He then becomes the unconscious bearer of these projections and his life will be dominated by the father's shadow. As the son acts out this shadow in the world, he becomes the embodiment of his father's shadow and he loses his own individuality. He is caught in his father's web, driven by an unconscious force. Or he may adopt a masculine persona similar to the father and become the obedient son, colluding with him further to repress the shadow. And so the power of the shadow is increased and can intrude on consciousness. Masculinity is split into an underground, sterile persona and an archaic, unconscious shadow, with the ego left fragile and defenceless, lacking the firm limitations set by a good father.

Daniel's father was a hero, a man who understood at some level that he had a gentle sensitive nature. A product of his time and culture, he imagined this was a negative thing and so he sought in every way possible to deny it. Believing that such a gentle and artistic nature wasn't masculine, he hid his sensitivity beneath a veneer of cool, clean detachment. He occupied himself by pursuing particularly masculine activities such as car racing and motorcycling. He had a bevy of male friends and he spent a lot of time with them. He did so at the expense of his family. Daniel's mother felt neglected, as did Daniel.

After his father's death, amongst his possessions, Daniel found a series of poems, written over a number of years. These poems recorded his life in a sensitive and lyrical way. No one had known about their existence. They surprised everyone and cast new light on Daniel's father's soul and his unfulfilled life. His frustrations, his disappointments and his incipient depression came to life in his poetry. His shadow spoke. Beneath the veneer of confidence and bravado lay the pieces of a fragmented and tortured soul whose exquisite sensitivity found living in the real world an ordeal. In the lines of his poetry, this man had allowed his soul to speak. That he had been ashamed of his sensitivity and his gentle heart was not only obvious, it was very sad. It had prevented him from opening up, from relating. Although he had many 'friends' these were all superficial relationships. No one had been close to him, even his wife and family. His shame about his sensitivity had crippled him by keeping him locked in isolation. In denying his soul, he had lost his family, and they in turn had been deprived of him.

Daniel is a poet. This doesn't sit well with him however. In some way, he has followed the unspoken bidding of his father's hidden soul. He has given life to an aspect of his father's shadow. But he can't quite square it with himself. Writing poetry does not really fulfil him. In a strange kind of way, he feels as his father did, that he is not totally grounded in himself as a man and as a poet. That in order to be masculine he should be out building roads or houses, or spending time with his male buddies in pubs, drinking. He prefers the company of women because he can express himself better with them. He likes to listen to them, he feels at home. He is not homosexual, but he cannot seem to form intimate relationships with women. Unconsciously, women threaten him because he fears that he is not strong enough in himself. He fears that if he were to have a relationship with a woman he would lose himself. He is so open he knows he would easily fall into the person to whom he opens his heart. Lacking the boundaries and the strength-making qualities that could help him feel safe enough to open up, he shies away from emotional commitment. So, his poetry is in that sense an escape and sublimation.

RECOVERING THE SHADOW

Daniel is living his father's shadow. He needs to recover his own in order to achieve a sense of balance and feel better about himself as a man. If a man remains at the stage of expressing the father's shadow, he is still blocked from the true expression of his own individuality. Once he finds and struggles with his father's shadow he will begin to mend the split and heal himself. In healing his father he empowers himself as a man. Discovering and reading his father's poetry is liberating Daniel. It liberates him because, by being exposed through his poems, his father's shadow is in the process of being recovered, being bought to consciousness. In this way, Daniel no longer needs to 'live out' his father's unlived life. It is living. He has found his father and now he can find himself.

Recovering the shadow is necessary in order to achieve balance and to restore wholeness. A father hungry wounded man must find and redeem the lost father from where he lies in the shadow. An archetype is neither negative nor positive. It is the attitude of consciousness that allots the archetype a negative quality and divides it in two. In the mutual casting of shadows, the unconscious tries to bring about a reunion of the split archetype. So, the father's shadow holds an essential missing part of the original wholeness of the masculine. In order for the collective image of the masculine to be healed and renewed, the rejected shadow must be integrated. As Robert Bly says, we must recover the Inner King. It is the shadow that keeps us fertile and potent, and often we need to free ourselves from the constraints of directed consciousness to experience this. In the dark, chthonic depths of the unconscious and nature we find the secret source of the masculine.

Jung himself was aware that he carried his father's shadow. Jim Fitzgerald discusses this referring to Jung's interview with Kenneth Lambert in 1950[8] where he spoke movingly of his own father complex... 'I had the whole problem of the father to solve'. Jung saw his father the Pastor as having to maintain a collective persona for his congregation. A Protestant pastor, Jung's father carried the persona of blind faith and belief in Christian teachings. It irritated Jung's intelligent and inquisitive mind that his father could never discuss the problem of belief. He would never question his beliefs, telling Jung that one should not think, but just believe. Jung felt this was wrong; that one should experience and know. Jung said 'Not until several years later did I come to understand that my poor father did not dare to think, because he was consumed by inward doubts. He was taking refuge from himself, and therefore insisted on blind faith.' Jung saw that his father was cut off from his inner self in a way that meant he dared not question external teachings. One gets a sense of Jung's father complex when he says that for him the father meant 'reliability and powerlessness'. He also pitied his father and recognised that he was a wounded man. He was wounded in that he represented the Christian ethos, which involves a wound to instinctual nature by elevating spirit and debasing instincts.

Notes

1.   P. Bloss, *Son and Father* in Fitzgerald, J. already quoted. P.2.
2.   G. Corneau, *Absent Fathers, Lost Sons*, p.37
3.   C.G. Jung, CW7 para 315
4.   C.G. Jung, CW5
5.   H.B. Biller, *Fatherhood:Implications for Child and Adult Development*. Handbook of Developmental Psychology, ed.Wolman, B. (1982)pp711-714
6.   G. Corneau, pp.19/20
7.   M.L. Von Franz, *Projection and Recollection in Jungian Psychology* Open Court, 1980
8.   C.G. Jung Speaking ed.McGuire,W. and Hull.RFC. (1980)
9.   Jung, C.G. *Memories, Dreams, Reflections* p.60

CHAPTER SIX

BLOOD OF THE FATHER

Every generation blames the one before
And all of their frustrations come knocking on your door
I know that I'm a prisoner to all my father held so dear
I know that I'm a hostage to all his hopes and fears
I just wish I could have told him in the living years

I wasn't sure there that morning when my father passed away
I didn't get to tell him all the things I had to say
I think I caught his spirit later that same year
I'm sure I heard his echo in my baby's new born fears
I just wish I could have told him in the living years

(Mike and the Mechanics 1988)

It is not enough however, to connect with the spirit of the father. To be properly incarnated, sons need to connect and identify with the instinctual, rooted nature of their fathers. A boy needs to connect with the blood of his father. He needs to connect with the physicality of his father's body in such a way that it feeds his own growth and development as a male. He will seek this in order to clothe his bones and draw his male soul into the world. In former times, male initiation rites served this purpose. Today in the West there exists no such initiations. In the absence of male initiation rites, how does a boy grow to be a man? How does he pass through the threshold from boyhood to manhood? When male initiation rites still guided the lives of men, a boy lived exclusively with his mother up to the age of nine or ten, when the initiating males arrived to take him away to a male enclosure. One could say that this point in his life marked his formal separation from his mother. And so he moved from his mother's house to his father's. I mean this in a symbolic sense of course.

Bly views the father/son connection in a particular way. He believes that values are passed on when two bodies stand close to one another, irrespective of whether they talk or not. He is referring to the close physical proximity of father and son, which has the effect of initiating the son into male adulthood. 'The pattern of father-and-son association set in the agricultural centuries amounted to constant labour close to one another, although there was often much emotional distance'. As already stated, today in the West, there is much evidence of father hunger, and nowhere is this felt more strongly than in modern father/son relationships. Bly writes that the average father in the United States spends ten minutes a day talking to his son, and he may not be standing close to him during those ten minutes. I know from my work with young men in particular, how deeply their need to connect with their fathers goes.

One young man spoke movingly of how his father's frequent absences from the family affected him. Describing his relationship with his father as 'formal', he was aware of a great need to connect with him on a more personal level. He was anxious for his father's approval so that he could secure his attention and his love, but he also feared him. He would ask his father to bring him back something whenever he went away. He missed him and he was eager to see him. When his father did not bring him back a gift, it hurt. Such a small thing one might think, but that gift meant so much. It symbolised his father's love; that his father was thinking about him. This boy was close to his mother, and his need to connect in a profoundly visceral way with his father was a necessary part of his journey to manhood.

MALE INITIATION

I understand what Bly means when he talks of the father/son connection in this physical way. I call it a connection to the blood of life. It is a kind of knowing that is physical, cellular if you will, and it has to do with that bone deep experience that comes from simply breathing, being there next to one another. A boy needs to connect with the blood of his father. He needs to do this so that he can inhabit the body and bones of his own male body in a comfortable way. Often this does not happen because modern society is structured in such a way that the father is often absent both physically and emotionally, and so his son is deprived. Men are then forced to feed their internal father hunger by joining various types of groups such as political parties or social and religious groups. Here in Ireland for example, I believe that the IRA and other political and ideological movements take the place of the father in many young men's lives. It is interesting to note that quite a number of IRA leaders are fatherless sons or second sons who could not inherit because of birth order.[2] It is not difficult to recognise in them the desire to replace and reclaim the missing father. Sports such as rugby and football are also a means of bonding between men. Male peer groups of all natures are ways of connecting with male/father energy.

In some societies, especially rural societies, fathers and sons work closely together doing physical things, walking together, farming, building, repairing machinery, cars and so on. Whenever this happens, Bly says, a vitamin like food passes from the father's body to the son's. It is almost like a physical transmission. Perhaps it is the case that transition from childhood to adulthood needs to involve such a physical transmission. As Bly puts it 'The son's body, not his mind receives food on a sort of cellular level, and the father gives it at a level far below consciousness.'[3] In this way, the boy gets some insight into what an adult masculine body is like. He learns the frequency that the masculine adult body vibrates to. Again, this is something he must learn for himself. He already has, from his time in the womb, a tuning to his mother's body, to her voice and to her essence.

Bly goes on 'During the long months the son spent in the mother's body, his body got well tuned to female frequencies: it learned how a woman's cells broadcast, who bows to whom in that resonant field, what animals run across the grassy clearing, what the body listens for at night, what the upper and lower fears are. How swiftly the son's body became, before birth and after, a good receiver for the upper and lower frequencies of the mother's voice! The son either tunes to that frequency or he dies'.[4]

After he is born, however, he will have to learn a new tuning. As he grows up alongside his father, he has the chance to retune to the male frequency. Whilst still in the womb the son is totally dependent on his mother, but after he is born he begins his journey away from her and toward father. The son needs to resonate to the father's as well as to the mother's energy. If he does not, something in him may not grow. Bly writes, 'boys who have not received this tuning or retuning will have a father hunger all their lives'. They may then spend the rest of their lives trying to find 'Father'. They will seek him elsewhere by joining male groups, clubs and so on, until they learn that they must find him inside themselves. Sometimes it is only as a result of enduring painful and traumatic experiences in their workplace and in their personal lives that they discover they have an absent father. These experiences may have such a profound effect on them that they may become extremely inward looking as a result. In the process of journeying within, they find father and they are transformed.

In *The Hunger for the King in a time with No Father*[5], Bly describes the modern phenomenon of the diminished father as making the longing for the inner king almost unbearable. I believe this longing to be at the root of many psychological problems in men and in society at large. I think it is time to redeem the father. I like to imagine that in some small way I am helping this process by focusing on the important role the father plays in the coming into being of his child. This focus highlights also the importance of having our men present and relating to us, not only when we go through the experience of giving birth, but as we try to love and to relate.

LIFE STRUGGLE

In male initiation rites, the father and other males sometimes inflict pain on the boy. The pain he endures symbolises the struggles of life and the fact that suffering is part of the human condition. It teaches the boy endurance. The goal of initiation is to strengthen the male ego. Mutilation, if it is part of the ritual, represents the expression of submission to the male principle.[6] The pain the boy submits to represents the end of the Mother's boy. The pain of endurance in the face of a life struggle represents an initiation into life. It gives meaning to suffering. In our modern, sanitised world, this is something we often lose touch with. We have grown used to seeking comfort and avoiding pain. We expect everything to run smoothly, and when we encounter obstacles we no longer feel that we have the inner resources necessary to overcome them. So we try to avoid them.

By creating a sanitised, pain-free life we become intolerant of suffering. If we feel pain, either physical or emotional, we all too easily run to doctors and therapists to be cured. The absence of meaning in pain and suffering is, in my view, in some way connected with the huge increase in suicides among young men in Ireland in particular. Young men it seems, choose to put an end to their pain by killing themselves. Seeing no purpose to their lives, and lacking the ability to overcome obstacles and suffer life's difficulties; faced with the threat of unemployment, the stress of modern life and the erosion of traditional values, death is their only recourse.

When the role of suffering is no longer understood in terms of helping us to grow stronger and to face life's challenges with courage, then we are faced with the spectacle of increasing number of young people running away from what they perceive as the horrors of the world. At a time when, paradoxically, treatment for mental illness and emotional pain was never so easily obtained, it is a great indictment of modern society that so many young men are taking their own lives. Suicide is the most radical action a human being can take to escape the pain of living. In a time of the 'absent father', could it be that these young men are seeking initiation like their primitive counterparts who learn to withstand pain and to master it so that they can become part of the world of men?

In Ireland the rate of suicide among young men is four times higher than among young women. There are, I imagine, many reasons for this. Perhaps one of the reasons is that nature initiates women and girls into suffering. In childbirth, for example, women are afforded the opportunity to suffer physical pain as part of life. Natural pain in general and childbirth in particular serve as an initiation. With menstruation and childbirth women are initiated into the 'blood mysteries' of the feminine. In the absence of male rituals, men have no such initiation. If they experience physical pain, most likely it will be as a result of injury or accident. In such circumstances there is no sense of natural pain or of suffering through it; and so, instead of experiencing it through their initiation rituals, they have to experience it through difficult or traumatic life events such as accidents, physical injury, bereavement, divorce, or redundancy.

The birth experience itself is an initiation.[7] It is an initiation into life. In male initiation rituals, the initiators give the boy the experience of being born again, this time to the father. Corneau describes it thus.[8] 'The Australian Aborigines re-enact the initiate's original birth. They build a tunnel of branches and bushes, twenty or thirty feet in length, and require the boy to enter into it. After a great deal of shouting and commotion, the initiate emerges from the other end of the tunnel, where he is welcomed with open arms and solemnly declared to be a man. He has been born through the body of a man; he now possesses a new mind and a new body.'

LEAVING HIS MOTHER'S HOUSE

Separation from mother is another very important feature of the male initiation ritual. It is up to the father to help his son do this successfully. As we have seen, sons need to identify with their fathers as a means of establishing their own male identity. This is extremely important. The father is essential for the boy's confirmation of his identity. And, as I have referred to earlier, it is the father who enables the boy to separate from his mother by intervening to break up the conspiracy between mother and son. A son who is deprived of his father's attention may be unable to advance into adulthood (psychologically). Many men in their 40s and 50s remain still bound to their mothers as if still in childhood. If there are no male initiators to take the boy away from his mother, it is left to the boy to do it alone. He may have reached middle aged by the time awareness of the conspiracy becomes sufficiently intense to enable him to break out of it. Initiations are intended to mark the son's separation from his mother and the world of his childhood and signal his new status as a man.

In the father's absence the mother's influence is heightened and the boy remains imprisoned in identification with mother. We know that for the child, the father is the first significant 'other'. His presence triggers a process of differentiation and heralds the end of symbiosis with mother. The child senses he is no longer the only object of desire. I believe it is very important for him to recognise this because often around this period in his development, rather than weaning himself away from the mother, he may begin to develop an over close bond with her instead. I have seen this happen particularly in cases where the mother's relationship with the child's father is distant or inadequate in some way. If the father is absent, a mother who is missing his male adult presence will quite unconsciously choose the boy to replace him. This is when the conspiracy between mother and son starts. Unfortunately it takes place at a time when nature dictates that they should be separating. It is my belief that this experience and the memory of the conspiracy may remain with the boy and surface later in his relationships with other women.

It surfaced in James's relationship with Isabel for instance. It was strongest whenever he found himself in situations when he felt trapped. On such occasions James saw his mother's face in Isabel; he heard his mother's voice and he felt her presence. Being over forty, a man approaching middle age and not a child, he recoiled from these images, but his heart was treacherous and led him back. Or perhaps it was the memory of almost forty years ago. However dim, it was still charged with energy and it propelled him towards her. He was as powerless to resist it, as the sea is powerless to resist the force of the wind. James felt himself shrink in size at such times, no match for his mother, or those aspects of his mother's character that he perceived in Isabel.

Marc too remembered the conspiracy with his mother in the deepest recesses of his memory and in every fibre of his being. He had been almost five years old when his mother had finally weaned him from her breast. Vaguely aware that his father was less important that he was in his mother's life, he had ceased to wonder why they never slept in the same bed. He had grown used to his own small corner of the big bed he and his mother shared. It was difficult to say at what point he had first become aware of his mother's frustration. Perhaps it was when he saw her gasp as they watched the love scenes in old movies as they sat curled up together on the sofa on a weekday afternoon. Or perhaps it was when he overheard her speak about her frustration with her husband to a woman friend. It also surfaced in his dreams. It was there in his desire to receive as a Christmas present a mini vacuum cleaner, so he could walk with her and lighten her burden. It was this conspiracy and his need to break it, which would lead him many years later to my consulting room.

SEX AND THE BODY OF THE FATHER

As we have seen, the identity of the son is also rooted in the body of the father. It is the father connection that helps the boy to establish not only his aggressivity but also his sexuality. The formation of a boy's sexual identity requires mutual idealisation between father and son. In other words, a love affair needs to develop between them. If the son is kept away from his father and a close physical relationship with mother is prolonged, this will often affect the son's sexual identity. Corneau suggests it will result in the son not developing positively in relation to his father's body, and developing negative ideas and images about his mother's body and against the female body in general. This is the point at which, he writes, 'the love story between the mother and the son turns into a power struggle, and the son begins his war against women'.[9]

The type of lover a man becomes subsequently very much depends on how he has been fathered. The Unfathered man may not be secure in his masculine sexual identity. Obviously this will affect his sexual relationships. If his transition to manhood has not included breaking away from his mother, the son may fear intimacy with a woman and he may seek intimacy with another man. Even if he is not gay, he may still be confused about his sexuality. He may be physically attracted to women, but emotionally, he may prefer the company of men. Perhaps he will have tried to love a woman but as he is terrified of losing himself, the relationship will have failed as a result of his fears and his inability to be truly intimate. Alternatively, he may relate sexually but will always hold a part of himself back, as though to deprive or punish his lover. She will sense this and it will confuse her. His lovemaking may become laced with the faintest whispers of misogyny. After lovemaking he will flee before any emotional demands can be placed on him. Fearing emotional attachments and the ties he imagines will be loosened by love, he will often leave a relationship after the initial stage. He will leave his lover hurt and bewildered. This man will be a 'walk away Joe', and a 'hole in the heart lover' destined to break many hearts. Emotionally he will not understand women. He will be threatened by them.

DON JUAN AND PETER PAN

An Unfathered man often becomes an eternal boy, a 'Puer', a Peter Pan refusing to grow up, someone who drifts from one thing to the next and from woman to woman never putting down roots. He may be the eternal seducer, the Don Juan who flits from woman to woman seeking more and more conquests and dropping each one as the novelty of the chase wears off. Addicted to the sensation of the first heady weeks of falling in love and seeking the ideal in each woman, his love evaporates when he discovers his ideal is not ideal after all but a normal, mortal woman with flaws. Psychologists have suggested that the eternal seducer is searching for the ideal mother. Corneau also wonders if the seducer is 'trying to recreate the original moment of grace when he lit up a woman's life by being born?' Is he attempting to recapture the time when he was perfect and divine to his mother and she to him?'

Difficult to answer any of these questions but easy to see that what the eternal seducer fears is true intimacy, especially in sexual union with a woman. His handsome charming manner may be alluring to many women but beneath that charm lies the heart of a scared boy, who fears losing himself if he gets to know a woman and lets her in. For this man, love loosens the boundaries of his heart once he gets past the conquest stage and so he will be unreliable in his love. However, the eternal seducer is doomed to come a cropper, usually at middle age, when he loses his charm and good looks and when cynicism and loneliness come knocking on his door.

Marc was like this. His early relationship with his mother was such that emotionally he remained with her, even when he became an adult. Drawn into the conspiracy against his 'absent' father at a very early age, he grew up with a secret fear. He feared women. Yet he desired them. More specifically, he desired their bodies. He was so fixated on his mother and her desire for him that unconsciously, he sought her in every woman he met. He became a Don Juan, drifting from conquest to conquest, never allowing himself to get emotionally involved. Addicted to the excitement and pleasure of sex, his sole aim was to get women to sleep with him. After a few weeks however, when the novelty had worn off, and he had got to know his lover, his interest waned. Imagining she was not the 'right' one, he would ditch her as soon as he got tired of her. He caused many of his lovers pain.

Somewhere in the deepest recesses of his heart, he was avenging his mother. His heart was cold. He could not love. His mother had claimed him and he had become a God. He imagined himself invincible and, like Icarus, he was totally out of touch with reality. His heart never opened. He never allowed himself to feel either the pain or the joy of loving. His only pleasure was sexual, and that was divorced from love. That is why he abandoned his lovers before he could become attached to them. Deep down in his boy's heart he feared emotional attachment, he feared love. He feared it because it would open him up and as a result he would then be vulnerable and out of control. When his lovers fell in love with him and made emotional demands on him, he fled. He feared both emotional commitment and responsibility.

Marc sought my help when the call of his soul became too strong for him to resist. Almost 38 years of age and unable to maintain a relationship for longer than a few weeks, he was aware of a need within him to experience something more. He was also aware of feeling a loss. He craved a relationship with a woman but he also feared it. In some distant place he also knew he wanted to connect with his father. In essence, he sought my help because he needed to break away from his mother in order to find a mate of his own. In therapy I symbolically became his mother, his lover, his father, his jailer and, finally, simply his analyst.

Our work was long and arduous. The most difficult part was the difficulty he had in committing to therapy and regular sessions. After the initial novelty of coming to therapy, he began to complain about the necessity of coming on a regular, weekly basis. He used many excuses to avoid committing himself to ongoing sessions. Work would get in the way, or money was short, and so on. Over time and with grim perseverance, we carved out a strong working alliance as well as a personal bond. The limitations of strict analytic procedures created strong boundaries that helped our work. Lacking a strong father and fearing an over powerful mother, Marc needed me to love him and allow him to love me, from a distance. The distance of psychotherapy and interpretation. Soul work. There were times when he experienced me as his jailer and as a stern father who kept strict boundaries and rules. He had to be there at the same time and in the same place three days a week. He needed this discipline. He needed to grow up. He had to mature into his male soul. Deprived of a strong father who could wrestle him away from the clutches of his mother, he projected father onto me. He felt restricted yet safe. Gradually over time he began to find and internalise a strong father. He found his inner father. Under his protection and with his newfound inner strength as a man, he was finally able to leave his mother's house and my consulting room.

CONFUSED SEXUALITY

When a man has not been fathered and has failed to make a secure transition to adult manhood, he may experience many fears around the issue of his sexuality. Often these will be unconscious fears. If he is sensitive by nature he will have been very influenced by his mother and the feminine principle. Male poets and artists, for example, are very much connected to their feminine intuitive side, which initially is tuned to mother's anima. The mother-son conspiracy is greater when the son is creative because his soul is open to feminine energy. His early impressions and experience of his mother will inform his own female side, his anima. If his father has not been strong enough to help him separate from his mother then he will fear his anima. He will fear being devoured by it, especially if he does not feel strong in his masculinity. Added to this, if the boy's father has repressed his own feelings and emotions, then the boy will carry his father's shadow into his own life. We saw this type of behaviour in the last chapter.

Confusion is prevalent in father hungry men. As referred to earlier, if a man's masculine identity is fragile he is often confused about his sexuality. This, coupled with his well-developed anima, may mean he has ambivalent feelings about the feminine side of his nature and women in general. The masculine and the feminine will not be balanced. Fear of homosexuality is one of the results of this way of being. This is because what we ignore forms part of our shadow and begins to exert an influence on us, intruding into our consciousness like an unwanted guest. A man whose masculine identity is fragile and who has been allied to a repressed image of the masculine, i.e. one without heart or feelings will fear these feelings in himself and imagine that he is gay. He will be horrified by the intensity of his feelings and his sensitivity. He will try and close the door of his heart, as he fears it will pull him into unsafe waters. To acknowledge his heart and his feelings as well as his physical senses means identifying with women and that makes him less of a man.

It has often been claimed that homosexuality is an expression of an unconscious search for the father and for a male identity. I suppose it is like a mirror image; you love what you recognise of yourself in the other. In mating with someone of the same sex you are also absorbing something of him or her. You are seeking to connect symbolically with something you possess in essence but have not yet actualised. It is also claimed that unconsciously, homosexuals are attempting to wrestle their bodies away from the clutches of their mothers.

When Peter came to see me, he was confused. Somewhere in his heart he knew that he was not gay, but at the same time he could not relate to women. He craved the affection and closeness of female company but felt inadequate in relation to his sexual potency. His mother had so dominated his father that he continued to feel very angry with her. He also had experienced her as very invasive and so he kept himself locked away as a protection from her. He hid himself and his feelings so much it was as if he had forgotten who he was. The energy tied up in keeping his mother at bay meant he had very little energy left over for himself. He was firing on three cylinders, as it were. When he was with a woman he feared not being 'strong' enough for her. He felt inadequate sexually, and this fear kept him from engaging fully with a woman. After a few failed attempts at relating sexually to women, he gave up. Should he turn to men? Was he gay? Would he ever be able to relate sexually to a woman? All these questions burned in his soul.

Peter was a gentle and sensitive man. His very strong, lean and masculine body appeared at great odds with his tender heart. His inner mother and father were out of balance. Within his psyche, his father was very small and sensitive, and his mother loomed large and domineering. As he lay on my consulting room couch he frequently became a baby, then a small boy. He needed to rage against his mother and yet simultaneously feel the gentle, caring affection of a loving mother. Some years later, he gradually learnt that he could have both. He could combine the gentleness of a loving and non-intrusive female who would allow him to grow up, with the strong assertive male energy he needed in himself. Peter grew into himself and discovered how to honour and love his sensitivity and his openness. Poetry flowed from his anima and he no longer fought against it. He felt stronger as a man. He began to meet women and consider having an equal relationship with them. His inner mother and father were now at peace. He flourished.

WHEN A MAN LOVES A WOMAN

An unfathered man, like any other man, will fall head over heels in love with a woman who represents his anima, his inner image of woman. She will have all the qualities he seeks in himself and more besides. Because he has a father hunger and does not regard himself as strong, his love will be characterised by a certain flavour and texture. When such a man loves a woman he may become tenuous in his love. As stated earlier, love loosens the boundaries of his heart so that he may fear losing himself. A man with a father hunger will attract a strong woman. She will draw out his strong male energy. He will attract her with the boyishness of his gaze and the softness of his inner soul.

Although outwardly strong, this woman will often house a wound in the softness of her own heart. Filled with idealism, she will clothe her lover in King's robes and when he doesn't fit them and her idealism takes a tumble, she will wonder what she has done wrong. More often than not, she will have done nothing wrong. Her lover, if he is a father hungry man, is a wounded man. By night he searches for his lost potency; by day he carries himself forward as a knight in shining armour. Seeking to hide his perceived inadequacies, he will build a protective skin around his sensitivities and carry on regardless, seeking to be a hero. For, there is no other route left for the unfathered boy. He must travel the road of the hero. He is never good enough for himself just as he is. He most certainly cannot be loved for himself. And so the will to achieve and shine takes the place of love in the boy's heart.

Someone once wrote that a man's need to be assertive and aggressive could be viewed less like an attempt to be superior and more an attempt to gain the love of a woman. I have found that often, deep in the heart of a man, lurks a primitive need to feel he has to win that love. If this is an archetypal impulse, it may partly derive from the boy's need to gain his mother's approval and love. On a wider scale, perhaps it is simply part of our ancient psychic priming in the same way that young boys dream of slaying dragons while young girls dream of being carried off on white horses. Despite everything, the ancient myths continue to dwell in the hearts of every man and every woman. Dream life and imagination is testimony to this fact. The hero whispers in every girl's heart as she silently entreats her lover to prove his love for her, while the will to conquer gleams as brightly as a flaming sword in the heart of a man in love. These myths live at night in the dreams of boys who fight as brave and valiant soldiers, and in the dreams of girls who see in the distance their knight in armour riding to take them away on white horses. Myths live within us as secret fires in our souls waiting to be activated by the right moment, the right experience.

James has a great need to love. He has a great need to be loved. His soul pulls him to experience this, but because his personality is weaker and hampered by his lack of fathering, he finds it hard. Having lost his father at an early age, and having been brought up in a relatively comfortable environment, he has never really had to struggle for anything. He has not been initiated. The hardship and struggle associated with entry into the male world was denied him, especially since his father was gone. An attractive man, James has no difficulty drawing women into his life. But because of his boyishness and his unconscious need to be 'looked after', he attracts predominantly strong women. Women who want to help him grow up and who expect things of him. When they do not get this, they grow tired of him and leave him. Most of these women want something more solid from James than he is capable or willing to give. James is still mother bound, which means he has not made a secure transition into the male world. He fears being controlled above all else. He both seeks structure (father) and he balks at it.

Isabel knew this. She saw it in the way he was difficult to 'pin down'. Perceiving control and pressure in perfectly ordinary situations, he was at times impossible to deal with. She wanted to love him and to feel his love, but their relating had a seesaw quality about it that exhausted her. For her own part, Isabel knew that at times she transferred her need for strong fathering onto him. She wanted him to be strong; she wanted him to fight for her, to be her knight in shining armour. She is a wounded woman searching for her saviour. She too has a great need to be loved. With James, often, too often, she was disappointed. He let her down so many times. She turned away from him in despair.

Isabel's ideal is to achieve the perfect union. The essence of this ideal is contained in the idea that the masculine takes the feminine out into the world because he loves her. This is the essence of the energy of the inner marriage. The marrying of the masculine and feminine principle within. Defined as a sense of wholeness, this is something we all aim to achieve. Jung called this the drive to individuate, to evolve into a sense of wholeness and balance. Individuation is the ultimate goal of analysis and therapy. Indeed it is the goal of life. All souls seek wholeness. The union of James and Isabel had difficulties because he was still seeking the father in himself. James had not connected to the blood of his father. This made him less than secure in the area of his sexuality and his maleness, and it complicated his relationships. And for Isabel, her father also was weak in that he had not been adequately embodied in her, and so she still seeks a man who will take her out into the world through love.

Notes

1.   R. Bly, in *Mother/Father* ed.by Wilmer, H. p.5
2.   Private communication from IIPSS (Irish Institute for Psychosocial Studies) Dublin
3.   R. Bly, in Mothers/Fathers ed. by Berry, P. p.2
4.   ibid.,
5.   ibid.,
6.   G. Corneau, *Absent Fathers, Lost Sons* pp146-147
7.   B. Mauger, *Songs from the Womb* p.100
8.   G. Corneau, *Absent fathers, Lost Sons* p.148
9.   ibid. p.23

PART TWO

FATHERS AND RELATIONSHIPS

CHAPTER SEVEN

SONS AND LOVERS

'While Stephen slept, his father watched him. The king's knight's pawn was in his son's hand, but his body had slumped backward in the armchair. Whatever move he had intended to make was frozen in his hand and the game lay suspended, its communication broken, like a missing page in an old love letter.'

(As it is in Heaven by Niall Williams)

Fathers have a particular influence on how a son develops as a lover and eventual partner. 'As it is in Heaven' is a novel which describes in beautifully descriptive terms, the soul connection between a dying father and his son. During a visit home, Stephen's widowed father learns that love has opened his son's heart. Without words, he enters into, and suffers with him the intricate tapestry of the pain and joy of love awakened. His own heart ravaged by the loss of Stephen's mother and young sister in a car accident some years ago, he fears for his son. Love would surely bring pain, perhaps greater than any human heart is capable of bearing.

'Philip Griffin watched him. He had watched him for thirty years, watched him more carefully than any father watched his son. He loved Stephen like a wall loves a garden. He knew that his son's life was lacking in excitement or joy, but believed that it needed to be fiercely protected from the treachery of dreams.' The silent and intangible love between father and son comes alive in the pages of this book. Often, the father's mark is thus subtle. His influence on his children is more mysterious perhaps and less tangible than that of their mother.

I once read that one of the greatest gifts a father can pass on to his son is the gift of how to love a woman. Perhaps this is a very moving way to describe some of the things a father brings to his son. There is no doubt that it is through our childhood eyes that we learn about love between a man and a woman. And because as human beings we love imperfectly, there are few of us who can say we received this gift. And even if we did receive it, it almost certainly was flawed.

A boy will form ideas on how to love a girl based on his experience of his father's relationship with his mother. Robert Bly has suggested, as we saw earlier in the book, that the receiving of impressions and the imprinting of values on children is not just a mental thing. It is also physical. But because it is much more common for mothers to be closely physical with their children since it is usually they and not the father who are the primary caregivers, it follows that women pass on their values much more so than men do.

In my work as a therapist I come across many instances where my adult clients report that 'an atmosphere' was felt and internalised by them during their childhood. Their parents might never have fought or been outwardly hostile to each other, but the child 'picked up' a disharmony. When there is harmony we feel it. It surrounds us like soothing background music. In disharmonious situations we feel tense and ill at ease. A child by and large picks up its mother's psyche and the imponderables in her soul much more readily than it picks up its father's, solely because of her proximity. Father is by nature more 'remote' than mother is in the early stages of a child's life.

Usually, both boys and girls will learn about love through their mother in the first instance. But since the boy must identify with father and break away from mother in order to grow into his own identity as a male, it is his father who really shapes him. It is not just his father's behaviour that will influence him, it is how his father feels and thinks about love. The boy will pick up quite unconsciously where love sits in his father's heart. He will sense the colour and taste of his father's love or the lack of it. If his father is a man who is wounded emotionally, then that will be transmitted to his son. If his father has a basic distrust of the feminine in general and women in particular, no matter how unconscious this distrust might be, the boy will sense this.

Conversely, he will also receive the positive and loving vibrations of his father's heart if his father loves, and is able to express his love for his partner/wife. The child will sense whether his father is confident and grounded as a lover and partner. He will also pick up his mother's happiness or unhappiness in a way that will affect him somewhere in his soul. The imponderables of parents' souls and their transmission to their children are very subtle processes. Children are in touch with the 'inside story' of life in general and their parents in particular.

DIVIDED HEART

One of the most insidious developments of modern life is the separation of the mind from the body. This kind of dualistic thinking means that feelings and the senses have come to be associated with the feminine in general and women in particular, while mind, thought or spirit belongs to the realm of men and the masculine. This divide has serious consequences for both men and women. It means that many of us fear love and emotional commitment, and it results in heartache. It often means that women alone carry the 'feeling' side of the relationships with men. This can become a great strain. In order to be healthy, love must be shared, passed between both partners like food. If one partner habitually holds back from expressing love, the other will feel deprived and compelled to probe for it. The more the one holds back the more the other reaches out. If the woman holds the emotional balance of the relationship, then a particular dance begins which often ends in pain. Since it is often the man who is 'out of touch' with his feelings, there is often an imbalance to start with. This means that many women are left with the task of grounding their partners in their bodies and their emotions. This places a huge burden on their relationships. It upsets the balance of energy, often causing power struggles between the partners.

As already stated, this body/mind divide for men often means that they will have a fear of their bodies and bodily needs and so for them sex often becomes divorced from love. Love is confusing for the man who cannot reach his heart because he has severed it in the mistaken belief that this makes him more of a man. And so women who love men who are holding back in this way, suffer. They suffer because it seems that they can go so far and no further.

As a hurt lover myself, I can identify with this dynamic. At some stage, as we relate, we will reach the border of their hearts guarded by the police of their defences, and we will silently and sharply be told to turn back. The more it seems we seek entry, the more we are deflected. And because intuitively we often sense what lies behind the border, it hurts all the more when we are pushed away. For we can feel their pain. Connected to our own hearts we will often sense and feel the devastation of their heartland and suffer the pain of not being able to help, and of being left abandoned.

Isabel's letter later on in this chapter describes it very well. Because a man's heart is often burdened by pain which he is not permitted to express without loss of face, he will keep it locked. Over time, the woman will stop trying and he will stop speaking. Eventually, lack of communication will lead to both partners clamming up and living behind their respective walls. All too often, the silence between them is so protracted it leads to permanent separation. They grow more and more apart until eventually and inevitably they part.

HURT LOVE

How do we learn about love? We arrive into the world with an innate capacity for love. Babies and small children, except in exceptional cases, are beings of light. Since they have not long left the spirit world, they still carry with them the memory of Divine love. As I have previously said, soul is very much in evidence in a new baby. How the child is received into the world however, will create a lasting impression. The human soul will be marked by its experience of life in the womb and afterwards. Whilst it is still in the womb, the child will be totally dependent on its mother, whereas after birth it will be open to various other influences. If a child's love is not accepted or acknowledged, or if it is not loved in return, then I believe it suffers soul loss. It begins to forget who it really is.

The seeds of distrust can be planted in the womb. Distrust makes it harder to love. The process of growing up in which we have to negotiate and interact with the world and with others gives form to our adult personalities. We know from psychology that if we are hurt early on in life, we will draw life experiences to us that have a similar tone, so that we can heal our hurt. I believe this is because the quest for wholeness is innate within us. Hurt or trauma, especially early on in life, causes a fragmentation of the soul. And the soul does not like to be divided. So if, for example, a boy experiences the loss of his father at a time when he needs him most, he will internalise this wound in such a way that later on in his life, the tone of the experience will be repeated so that he has a chance to heal it. This might mean that as an adult he will experience the loss of a loved one, which will force him to deal with his previous loss. Loss can appear in many guises, and so it might be that he loses an important job, a house or property, his marriage, or anything that will make him face up to the impact that his first loss had on his life.

James lost his father when he was barely seven years old. He never mourned him. Consequently, he now has a deep fear of loss, which prevents him from getting, too attached. He fears true emotional commitment; he has a heart wound. As luck would have it, in later life he again experienced this loss in many guises. The break up of his marriage, the loss of his home, and, finally and most tragically, the death of his son. It is as if life attracts like a magnet that which most needs healing in our souls. As long as we remain unconscious of our wounds, they will continue to pull at us. Only now, in middle age, is James beginning to wake up to consciousness. As he comes into awareness he has a chance to heal. Souls draw us into awareness, whether through physical symptoms, relationships or life events. James has lived so long with his buried heart wound that his mistrust has become deeply internalised. He even mistrusts himself. He searches to retrieve himself in the lost fragments of his soul. His personal challenge is to trust.

WOUNDED HEARTS

Today, at a time when marriages and relationships are breaking down at an unprecedented rate, one is likely to encounter many wounded lovers. In a poem entitled Wounded Lover I write about my experience at a time when I was suffering the pain of loss and betrayal in love.

You came to me with wounds of love
My own reflected and intensified
Three women had filled your heart
And taken part of you away
You lost a father, a son, and your own life seed
I saw you reduced and hurt
My soul mate, lover and eternal friend
The hardened earth in which you had placed your seed
Each time rejected you
Until at last, exhausted, you gave up
Your heart built a skin around itself
To protect its tenderness.

As you lay down your golden head behind the wall
You had built
You closed the door
Vowing never to love again
Until
Until I came along and refused to leave
Becoming sentinel to your heart
Drawn by the magic we had created
So quickly and so unexpectedly.

If a man has a secret heart wound and he is challenged strongly enough to heal it, then inevitably he will be drawn to a woman with a similar wound. They see mirrored in each other that which most needs healing in them. It takes great courage to accept the challenges that the soul sets up for us. We enter relationships because, consciously or unconsciously, we want to grow. Our soul guides us there. And so our relationships are not always easy, for it is in them that we are often guided for healing. It is generally our inner child, activated by our relationships that uncover our wounds. We want our partners to be different, to meet our needs, to be there for us, no matter what. Often we are disappointed because they let us down and they turn out to be not what we expected. If we refuse to look within and continue to remain unaware, we may desert them in the belief that we have made a mistake and that we can find what we need in another person.

We continue seeking in vain. For we need to learn that what we seek in the other person is, in fact, what is lacking in ourselves. That in essence is what 'falling in love' is. We fall in love with a lost part of ourselves that we perceive in the other person. For a man it is his anima, for a woman it is her animus or inner man. Our beloved will embody all the qualities we desire and the energy of our soul at that time. He or she will represent everything our soul desires.

Sometimes however, we are so blinded by our idealism we cannot see what is before our eyes. When the light of our blind love fades and we begin to really see the person we have invested with such adoration, our idealism takes a tumble and he or she falls from God or Goddess to ordinary mortal complete with flaws. The ordinary mortal will disappoint us. We will miss the elevated feelings of loving a King or Queen. Even Kings and Queens house an inner child and this child with all its wounds and insecurities is bound to surface in the course of a relationship. Our inner child may be wounded in a particular way, and in the course of relationship, it will be reawakened to its need for love as well as to its wounds. If we remain ignorant of our own inner needs, we will quickly become disillusioned with the work involved in maintaining a relationship and understanding the needs of the other person. Awareness and connection with our inner child is necessary in order to heal these wounds and maintain healthy, loving and harmonious relationships.

Isabel, nursing her own secret wound of loss and abandonment, was almost inevitably destined to meet and mate with James. Both of them were searching for the lost part of themselves. Although she could not see it, since it was she who usually pushed for resolution in their relationship, she was being challenged by her soul to trust. Her early life was constructed in such a way that, there was no certainty, no structure, no person she could rely on. Dragged into the world in the middle of the night when she had been in the womb barely seven months, she felt alone. She was alone. And James too was alone.

Whenever she was apart from James, Isabel became overwhelmed with fears that he would leave her. If he did not call, she imagined that he no longer loved her. She is, one would say in psychological terms, 'insecurely attached'. And since James mistrusts himself, he feared he would not meet her needs and he would not be there for her. This fear of inadequacy made him pull back. Moreover, he resisted becoming too attached because deep down he feared that he would lose her and so reawaken the unbearable pain of loss in his heart.

THE LOVE DANCE

When a wounded man meets a wounded woman, something profound takes place. An ancient, hidden wound is reopened and seeks to be healed. With the flames of love, the archetypal battle between man and woman is activated and stirs in the hearts of both of them. The woman who loves a father hungry man will want to help him grow. Somehow she will have sensed that he is searching for father, that there is a part of him as yet unborn. If inside her heart she also has a father wound, she will project much of this need onto him. She will seek to root him, to bring him into life. He, attracted to the strength in her that he seeks for himself, will fall into the magic she creates with its unique combination of female beauty and the intoxication of sex and power. Together, they will begin the dance of love. Often, the strange intermingling of love, power and surrender will draw them both into a particular kind of rhythm where each will play a part already destined by the complicated legacy of their respective family histories.

In the relationship dance, when the excitement of the initial attraction fades a little, long repressed images emerge from the dark corners of their souls to join the dance, thereby altering the rhythm. She may find that beneath his cool and handsome veneer, lies the heart of a scared boy or a misogynous dictator. He may discover that behind the allure of her beauty and sensitivity lurks a frail, insecure girl child or a trapped mother witch. As these inner characters join the dance of love, the rhythm becomes more complex. Individually the partners will be challenged by the unfinished business of their childhood and their souls. In the complex mixture of feelings involved in relating, each partner will have to untangle the knotted threads of their own lives in such a way as to achieve their individual freedom. Often this does not happen of course, and some relationships do not survive the storms that are stirred up by the past.

The father hungry man unconsciously seeks structure but he also resents it in his partner/wife. Therefore he may try to escape what he perceives as the confines of her needs as well as the confines of the relationship itself. At the very least he will be fearful of commitment, for commitment means being there, for better or for worse. It means making a choice and taking responsibility for that choice. It means 'growing up'. She will sense his reluctance to commit and she will suffer each time he pulls away. When this happens, it feels to her as though he has turned her into a dragon that wants to bind him. Mistaking love and emotional commitment for loss of power, this man will imagine that in order to take his own power he must assert himself against her. She will then become the mother from whom he must break away in order to grow into a man.

When this happens, she will feel rejected, and the loss of him will become an ache in her heart. Her wonderful lover has now become a boy, and boys should not mate with their mothers. Nursing the tenderness that love has opened in her heart, she will mourn her lover, and when her crying is over, ever so subtly she will close off the corners of her heart to him. A wall will be erected between the lovers, so that when the dance changes and they come together again as they inevitably do, the work of dismantling the wall covers the magic that is love. Isabel's letter tells us something of this.

ISABEL'S LETTER

Isabel sat for a long time after replacing the receiver. James's phone call had upset her. Waves of anger swept through her. These she could expect because it was the usual type of family argument about arrangements and dates. What she did not expect however were the big tears that rolled down her face and landed plop on her computer keyboard. Appalled, she looked down at the offending droplets as if to defy their very existence. But soon they became lost in a sea of tears and she could no longer see. All over her desk lay crumpled pieces of paper on which she had begun her letter and which frustrated, she had subsequently discarded. Isabel pulled out her pen and yellow pad and wrote:

Dear James,
I write in great distress, having just put the phone down. The truth is your phone call has finished me...I guess it is the last straw. I never could have imagined the depth of the pain that would take shape in me, formed out of the icicles of your words. My heart, so recently wounded, had opened to you

gently. Not thinking, I gave my love unguarded. Though never formed in words, your love surrounded me with light, and my heart sang to be with you. You walked with a spring in your step and your tender heart took one step forward. Your soul and mine held hands, and I felt the poetry of love surround us. But just as quickly as it came, it suddenly disappeared; and darkness took its place. In that place of darkness there is no sound. There is no love. There is nothing only emptiness and the pain of loss. Far away in the distance are two walls. Inside one wall you rest, having taken refuge from the storms of the heart. Behind the other I crouch, fearful of being seen, also resting from the storm. I crouch because at those times, in the heat of the storm, my spirit feels crushed and my wings get damaged. I crouch because I am waiting for my wings to mend before I can fly again. You, for your part, do not crouch. You stand immobilised by the heavy armour you assume each time you feel the slightest threat of hurt.

Between these two walls is that place of darkness, the valley of fear, where each is afraid to tread. Who will cross the divide and approach the other? Usually it is me who does the approaching. Is this because I have more courage? Or is it because I have less fear? Perhaps it is because I am more foolish and more in love. Who knows? What I do know is that I am now worn out. I am worn out by the emotional turmoil that loving you causes me. I am tired of always crossing the great divide alone. I am tired of 'giving in' in order to win you around. You talk a lot about your own hurts. Well I am very hurt too and I am just so sensitive, so sensitive that each time this happens it tears an extra strip off my heart and I just want to give up. Why can't you come forward for a change? Why can't you come to find me?

We are not new to this. We have travelled this road many times before together, and each time the storm rages we take flight and then take refuge behind our respective walls. It is time to change, to find a new way, to travel a different route. It is time to offer each other a hand. Two people crossing the great divide can meet in the middle and therefore each covers less ground. Two souls are stronger than one. Two hearts, no matter how wounded can form a whole and mend.

Yours,
Isabel

Isabel folded the letter and placed it in an envelope ready for the next day's post. She gazed at it lying there next to her computer and resisted the temptation to take it out of its envelope and read it again. She had already read it twice. 'Don't be ridiculous' she scolded herself for being so pathetic. A common occurrence these days. Though she'd known for a long time that she was blessed with what seemed to be an extra tender heart, she never tired of beating herself up over it and wishing she'd toughen up. She got up from her desk and went to bed.

JAMES AND ISABEL

Isabel was a woman in her late 30s who had suffered a marriage break-up several years previously. She had been in therapy several times before she met James, and was very psychologically and spiritually aware. This awareness and the fact that she was no stranger to soul pain did not prevent her from falling into the usual relationship difficulties. Creative and articulate, her romantic nature pulled her into experiencing the highs and lows of a passionate relationship with a man who was destined to disappoint her. Melancholia was part of her nature, and when things did not work out, she would get distraught. Relating to James forced her true nature out into the open, and since he often could not respond to her emotionally, she was thrown back on herself again and again. Writing was how her soul expressed and healed itself. Her letter is evidence of this.

James was a very different personality. He was 43 years old, and had also been married. James, people thought, lived a charmed life. Good looking and blessed with a sunny personality, everybody loved him. Women fell in love with his charming manners and style, his gentleness, his quiet calm and good nature. Only Isabel knew the dark corners of his soul. Only she knew how sometimes the fog that comprised his inadequacies and lack of self-belief would cover him so that the sun stayed away. Isabel, who loved him, knew that in the quietness of rest, there was no rest for James who tortured himself with thoughts of his perceived failures and multiple fears. At such times this handsome and well built man shrivelled to an apprehensive boy of barely seven years old, a boy who had lost his father in the middle of the night. A boy who was frightened and bewildered and who, lacking the space to cry, gradually erected a hero's wall around himself. A boy who very quickly learnt not to show his true feelings and went around cheering people up.

And then there was Isabel. Isabel was beautiful. She had brains too. 'Brains to burn' her friends thought. Or rather her friends' parents thought as they watched her outstrip their academic performance at university, with seeming effortlessness. Isabel had always possessed a good brain. At school the nuns despaired of her behaviour which was undoubtedly rebellious, but they comforted themselves with the certainty that she would do very well in her exams, something that would make the school look good. She never seemed to put in that much effort, much to the disgust and envy of others in her class who spent hours swotting over texts. 'You have a photographic memory' she was told when, yet again, she came first in Geography and stood up in the class to recite her Latin texts.

But there was always something defiant about Isabel that made the nuns mutter amongst themselves and wear an almost permanent frown. She had wild, golden hair and her big brown eyes were set in a face that seemed too small to accommodate them. You never knew what she was thinking, and her eyes had that far off look of one who sees beyond the every day. Perhaps it was her restless soul, or the fact that she was born beside the sea in the middle of the night when she had been in the womb barely seven months, no one knew for sure, but Isabel had a wild streak which anyone who came in close contact to her knew better than to try and tame.

James and Isabel had met by chance. A friend at a social gathering introduced them. Fairly innocuous you might say, but there was nothing innocuous about it. For James and Isabel were as destined to meet as the sun sets in the West every evening. To all outward appearances, they were not right for each other, they did not have a lot in common and they mixed in different circles. Isabel was more spiritually inclined; James was by some accounts, an Epicurean. And yet there was a strange pull of fate to their relationship. It was as though they were meant to be. There was a familiar soul connection evident in they way they related. Neither wanted a relationship, both were on the rebound from previous affairs that had hurt them. Both were on the defensive, especially Isabel, who was still nursing an old love wound.

The inevitable happened, for it is an unwritten law that whatever we fear most and try to avoid will happen because we will attract it to us like a magnet. For Isabel and James there seemed to be no choice in the matter. Both were pulled by a force that seemed to have nothing to do with them.

Isabel succumbed first to her destiny, despite her misgivings about entering into a relationship that was to tear her apart. A soul-destined relationship in which she would experience love such as she had never known. And pain, frustration and hurt. There were times when she wished she had never met him. When they were together the intensity of their relating tore at her heart, as agony followed ecstasy. When apart, the hunger to be together pulled at her soul until it became a relentless ache. She had no answers. She suffered.

For James it was no less intense, but lacking the emotional vocabulary to express himself, and fearing emotional involvement because of the pain and confusion it threw him into, he resisted. He had always flown from emotion. He disliked feelings, not because he felt little, but because he felt too much. Although equipped with a strong and capable veneer, inside he was soft and easily hurt. Indeed he was so easily hurt you would sometimes be afraid to speak your mind in case he took offence. Isabel knew this. She knew that inside the tough hero's robes he liked to wrap himself in lay the tender wounded heart of a hurt boy. Never successful in love affairs, and having endured a broken marriage, James closed the doors of his heart with a sigh, vowing never to love again. Love, he believed, doesn't work. It only hurts. He didn't realise that with those words and sentiments he had locked himself into a prison of his own making. He was fond of seeing himself as a victim and that in itself kept him locked in an infantile place where he didn't need to take responsibility. It was his single dark and most pervasive fault and the cause of much heartache for those close to him. There weren't many of these people, because James allowed few if any to get close to him.

When Isabel danced into his life that winter's evening, he was catapulted into a world that both fascinated and frightened him. He wanted to run yet he was drawn to her as a moth to a flame. She awakened feelings in him that he'd long thought buried. She pulled at his heart in a way that left him shattered and bruised. And yet, there were times when she flowed with him, blending into the same soul wave. Their energies simply and gently swirled over and into each other. Their youthful natures were eminently compatible. They got along well. Their creative energies blended and they worked well together.

But at other times, on those occasions when they argued, or when something made him feel trapped, he hated her and he hated the relationship. When James felt this way, Isabel's love created demands that appeared insurmountable. Her love and her need for him made him feel stifled. Claustrophobic, he would seek freedom. Freedom then meant running as far away as possible. He described freedom as being 'above and away'. He wanted to soar free as a bird. His passion entrapped him, as did his fear of emotional commitment. After a fight, sometimes he recalled Isabel standing where he'd abandoned her, and he felt as powerless to stop his heart from lurching towards her, as he was to stop the shutters came down with a clang against her. He turned away. James was good at distracting himself. Always an active man, he enjoyed his work and had many friends.

Isabel suffered. She loved James but she could not understand the complex nature of this love, or the man she had given her heart to. At times she reached well beyond the borders of the wall he had erected long ago around his heart, and their relationship flowed with the ease that accompanies true lovers. But on a great many more occasions she came up against the massive borders both of them had built to protect themselves from the strong tides of emotion and longing that threatened their survival. When he withdrew from her, she pushed forward, reaching with her hands outstretched for the love he appeared to be withholding. The more she pushed, the more he withdrew. Eventually, exhausted, she would pull back, folding her arms around her body as if to protect herself from losing any more precious energy.

Afterwards she would spend long days, sometimes weeks without contacting him. She wouldn't return his calls, and often she asked him to stop phoning. He lived then in her dreams, though in her fevered state she resented even these. Her energy withdrew from the relationship; she sought protection from him. She felt him to be emotionally sapping of her. She wanted someone better.

These episodes confused James. Alerted by the change in tempo, when Isabel retreated, invariably he came bounding back. Her emotional withdrawal eased the pressure he often felt in the relationship. In the space created by her moving back, he realised he did not want to lose her. When she withdrew, he could not stop himself from seeking contact. He rarely allowed three days to go by without phoning her. He missed her. But that was not all. With horror, he realised he needed her. He stepped forwards.

And so the tide of their relationship came and went.

'YET EACH MAN KILLS THE THING HE LOVES.'[1]

Both Isabel and James are casualties of lost or broken love. This made them at times fearful and mistrustful, and it lent a particular flavour to their way of relating. When we are hurt in love we often unconsciously behave in ways that will test and sometimes destroy the one we love. At some level, the hurt part of us feels un-loveable and so we have difficulty accepting love when it comes our way. We lack trust. James feared failure and the disclosure of his inner life, which housed a weak and shameful man who was unable to face the world. James imagined this, knowing that somewhere deep inside rested the tender broken heart of a wounded boy. Fearful of rejection, he was afraid to reveal himself as he really was. He assumed the cool veneer and persona of a soldier, capable, emotionally detached and practical.

Isabel, with an inner world ravaged by loss, devastated by her failed marriage and lost love, had long since given up any notion that true love existed. If it did exist, it was not something she could ever rely on. Isabel had by now turned love into an ideal. It existed in her dreams and she gave voice to it in her poetry, allowing the words to take on the mantle of romantic love. In real terms, she feared love above all else. Expecting hurt and abandonment, she pulled back when the possibility of love was near. When it came along, she often did not recognise it, so blinded was she by the light of her idealism.

Many people today suffer from a sense of failure in love. Broken marriages and families torn asunder are such an increasingly common feature of modern life, that young people have become cynical about marriage and families. Reared on a diet of arguments and hurt between parents, they grow up with a fear of commitment. 'Marriage doesn't work, look at our parents'. Most parents who split up feel guilt in relation to their children. The call of nature is very strong, and for many of us creating a family is the strongest call of all. If the structure and the fabric of the family we have created is ruptured, then we will inevitably feel that we have failed. It will make us tentative about starting a new relationship and creating a new family.

Nonetheless, perhaps in an attempt to recreate and 'make good' a broken family, many people embark on second relationships and remarriage quite quickly. Sadly, however, statistics show that the failure rate for second marriages is even greater than for first marriages. Perhaps this is because second marriages often take place soon after the break up of the first, before proper resolution of underlying conflicts has taken place. Marriage or long-term relationship break-up is a serious matter and it takes time to recover from the emotional turmoil involved. Many people embark on second marriages for the wrong reasons. Some simply do not want to be alone and they will compromise their integrity for the sake of being in a relationship. Others cling to the ideal of marriage and parenthood and imagine that in order to be good parents they must marry again in order to provide their children with a stable home.

Research shows that men do less well than women when a marriage breaks up. Perhaps this is why it is common for men to venture forth into other relationships straight away. Divorced or separated women tend to cope better alone. I imagine this has something to do with the fact that most men do not have emotionally intimate relationships with other men coupled with the fact that Western culture equates masculinity with a toughness that involves repressing emotions. For the man then, the only emotionally intimate relationship he often has is with a partner. With her he may talk about his feelings, open up. I see this in my own practice, where men by and large prefer to consult a female therapist, believing they can open up more easily with a woman. In today's emotional climate, in order to remain open and emotionally aware, men appear to need women. When they lose them, they can be left emotionally isolated. With no one to talk to about their feelings, they often enter a wasteland filled with loneliness.

SILENT SONS

Right now a great many fathers are passing on to their sons a silent but perceptible sense of failure in relation to love and marriage. A son will pick up his father's pain whether he expresses it or not. He will also pick up his mother's pain. However, it is from his father that he will learn about love from a man's perspective. If he sees his father as weak or 'broken' in some way, this will define his own sense of himself as a male. In the break up of a home and a marriage, much is determined by the way the father leaves the marriage. I am reminded of the words of a well-known song. 'I remember the day my father walked out; He left with a whimper not with a shout...' This son perceived his father as emasculated. Equally he may perceive his father as the aggressor and his mother the victim, in which case he may feel a great deal of anger towards his father. The way in which the children perceive the parents is the most important issue.

In a marriage break-up, children usually take sides. Many will feel rejected and abandoned by their fathers, as it is more common for the man to leave the family home. I know from my work that all young children, deep down, would prefer their parents to remain together. Again this appears to be in nature's way. The expectation of having a mother and a father is an archetypal priming affecting all human beings. As parents I think we recognise this at some intuitive level, and so it increases our sense of guilt. In a marriage break-up, boys (and girls) will often experience the loss of their father (or mother) as a betrayal and abandonment. If there are visitation rights, some will imagine that father is only doing his duty when he takes them out on the allotted day. The phenomenon of the 'McDonalds' father is a sad but inevitable feature of modern life. It is very poignant to see a father spending a few short hours with his children in a public place simply because he has nowhere else to bring them.

Joe felt the loss of his father very keenly after the split up of his parents' marriage. He recalled his feelings of pain when, as a little boy of nine years old, his father came to collect him on the day allotted by the courts. Hoping for a relationship with his father, he was bitterly disappointed when instead he brought him straight to his girlfriend's house and left him there to play with her children, who were also fatherless. He felt abandoned and rejected. He had no time with his father alone and, on top of that, he had to endure his father's girlfriend while his young heart was filled with complicated feelings about protecting his mother. Joe's father was simply unaware of all this. He did not intend his son any harm.

It is generally accepted that after a marriage has broken up, both mother and father should introduce a new partner to their children very slowly and with a great deal of discretion. Where the father has left home, children need an exclusive relationship with him. For a boy it is crucial for his future as an emotionally functioning man and father.

As an adult, Joe now realises that his father was emotionally unavailable to him because he himself was broken. His father had great difficulty coping with feelings and expressing them. He was emotionally needy and so he headed straight into another relationship for comfort. Despite knowing this, adult Joe feels a great deal of anger for the little child Joe who lost out. He needs to feel this in order to heal the father wound inside him. Joe's father had probably unwittingly put his own emotional needs before those of his son. To please his father and gain his approval, Joe had very little choice but to accept the situation as his father presented it. He also tried to 'love' or get on with his father's girlfriend. This was hard for him since he saw her as his mother's replacement. He repressed his true feelings and protected his father.

Joe internalised many feelings in relation to family, love and marriage. Some of these were conflicting, as the basic need to recreate family and find love with a partner jostled with the reality of what he himself had experienced as a child. He was confused about the heart of the father. His perceptions of his own father's heart; his unexpressed fears and inability to express love verbally or physically, sat uneasily with the reality of his father's obvious needs in relation to love. Added to all of that, Joe had resentful feelings about how his father treated his mother. Did he ever love her? If so, then why did he leave her? He also had a fear of failure, particularly in relation to becoming a lover and father. He had picked up on his father's deep sense of failure and this added flesh to his own budding masculine development.

A man with a frail masculine identity will fear failure above all else. If he fails, or feels he will almost certainly do so, he will turn his face away from battle rather than to be seen to fail. The drive to succeed is, I believe, drummed into boys and men, and it is rooted at a deep archetypal level. It is perhaps the remnants of an archaic warrior energy and part of the endowment of the masculine principle. Some men, often wounded and father hungry men, are afraid to become lovers and fathers. 'Better to have loved and lost' is not something that sits easily on their shoulders.

HEART OF THE FATHER

And so to the heart of the father. There is much evidence that in today's modern world, the heart of the father is very wounded. I mean this on both a personal and a collective level. It is not only the heart of the personal father but also the heart of the collective father that influences us and informs us in our love relationships. In later chapters I will describe how this wounding is activated and given expression as a result of the huge upsurge in broken marriages and relationships, and how difficult it is to love at a time of broken heart. For just as the personal father influences and imprints his son, so the collective father imprints our consciousness about love and relating.

Nowadays, people are finding it difficult to maintain intimate relationships. This means that loneliness and emotional alienation are on the increase. Despite a growing psychological and spiritual awareness, heart or soul wounds abound. The huge growth in mind/body/spirit consciousness is witness to the quest to heal the human soul. Most bookshops are full of books on how to achieve and maintain emotionally fulfilling relationships, on how to heal broken hearts, and on how to live emotionally healthier lives. Most of us know that in order to heal our souls and to become whole again, we must be reconnected with what we have lost.

The heart of the father will be healed once the balance

between internal and external masculine and feminine energies has been achieved. As within, so without. In my work as a therapist I know that I am merely facilitating the reunion of these forces in the souls of my clients. It is when a man recovers his connection with his anima that he begins to heal the wounded heart he has worked so hard to hide. His anima incorporates his ability to relate both to himself and others by forming a bridge between opposing forces. His anima is his soul image and without her he lives in a dry, unfeeling place.

One of the ways through which a man can reconnect with his anima and his ability to love, is through becoming a father. Loving his children and letting them love him can open the heart of the father.

Notes

1.   Oscar Wilde, *The Ballad of Reading Gaol*

CHAPTER EIGHT

DESPERADOS

'Desperado, why don't you come to your senses
You've been out riding fences for so long now.. '

(The Eagles)

'I WANTED you to be there for me', Eileen spoke as if
addressing me, but I knew what she meant. She was actually
addressing Robert, her former husband. She was in pain and
she had sought my help in dealing with some of the unresolved emotions surrounding her marriage and the birth of her
children. Eileen was an attractive, elegant and articulate
woman in her late thirties. She was also a recovering alcoholic. Despite her consistently immaculate appearance, she
was in chaos. Her inner world was a mass of murky and tangled feelings, and I had grown used to looking beyond her
external appearance to the rawness of her 'inner child'. In my
consulting room she wore an almost permanent frown, the
only outward sign of unease in an otherwise pretty face.
Talking about her pregnancies stirred up all sorts of things for
her. It brought back memories of the disappointment and pain
she harboured as a result of what she perceived as her failed
marriage. She and Robert had three pregnancies, one of
which, the last, conceived only six months before the break up
of the marriage, had ended in abortion. Now, four years later,
Eileen was reliving that painful period during her therapy sessions with me.

'I never really wanted an abortion', she said, 'But I
couldn't see how I could have the baby when Robert wasn't
really in the marriage'. She began to cry. I encouraged her to

go on, to speak to Robert, to open her heart and to say all the things she had kept locked inside for a long time.

'Where were you? I was so proud to be carrying the baby, our child, the fruit of our renewed love, our union. But you were not there. You were elsewhere, occupied it seems with your leisure pursuits, your mates'. She continued: 'What did I ever do to drive you away? All I ever wanted was your love. I was angry with you because you weren't there for us, the family. We needed you. But you, blinded by the attractions of life outside our marriage, never saw me, never felt me, never knew that all I wanted was you to be there'. Eileen could no longer contain herself. Heavy deep sobs erupted from deep inside her.

My heart went out to her. I knew how much she had loved Robert and how much she loved her children. I knew that creating a happy and harmonious family was very important to her. In her anguish I heard the raw pain of the child, the little wounded girl who wants Mummy and Daddy to be happy, and who longs for a joyful and peaceful family. Eileen was one of four children, and an only daughter. With an alcoholic father and a stern, cold and emotionally unavailable mother, she walked into marriage early in her life, probably in an attempt to secure the love she had failed to receive as a child. She did not find it.

The search for love takes us down many roads, and often it leads us into a wasteland, although we don't realise this at the time. This is because when we are emotionally wounded, we are often blinded by our search for love. We go looking for it in places where we are unlikely to find it. If we have not experienced being loved as children, then more often than not we lack the emotional vocabulary that would enable us to encounter and harness love in adult life. We may then end up trying to secure it at a cost to ourselves. We may choose unsuitable partners for example. Partners who are unable to express their love for one reason or another, and who are destined to disappoint us. When we are wounded in love we commonly tend to compromise ourselves in order to be loved.

Eileen met Robert at university, when she was nineteen and he was twenty-one. They were full of the idealism of youth. He was a gentle, sensitive type of man, who had cultivated a veneer of detached, cool confidence. At that time, his reticence and the tight reign he kept on his soul's longings, attracted Eileen who was much more emotional by nature. She saw him as a challenge. She also liked his refined character and his charming manners. A fiery redhead with a much more vibrant personality, she would affectionately call him 'my reserved soldier'. To Robert, Eileen was all the things his soul longed for. She was not only beautiful, she was vital, alive. Indeed, to Robert it felt as though she was more alive than anything or anyone he had ever known. She fascinated him.

They had a brief courtship and were married within eight months. Eileen was already expecting their first child. It was after the birth of Conal that the first ghosts began to appear in the partnership. Ghosts from both their pasts, danced into their marriage and gradually assumed the proportions of demons. In Eileen's case, it was the ghost of her father. For Eileen had a very deep father hunger. Her father had been 'absent'. He had been physically present but not emotionally available. A man with a gentle nature, it seemed he felt himself incapable of being either a good father to his children or a strong husband to his wife. At some level he appeared to be weak and helpless. He was no match for his feistier wife.

Eileen's mother was a strong 'matter of fact' woman. She coped with her disappointment at not having a strong husband by dominating him. Totally disempowered, Eileen's father took refuge in the pub, along with his friends. There is no doubt that he loved his little daughter, but he may have felt he could not reach her or relate to her because his wife claimed her, as she did all her children. The more her husband was absent from the marriage, the more Eileen's mother became demanding and controlling. The marriage between Eileen's parents took on a particular but also very common psychological dynamic within which their children were caught. Eileen's father became the eternal youth, a Peter Pan to her mother's Devouring Witch. The more she sought from him the more he withdrew. He felt her as demanding, the mother witch who sought to trap him. She felt him as immature, unavailable and irresponsible.

PETER PAN AND MOTHER WITCH

The marriage of Peter Pan and the Mother Witch is doomed to failure however, for it ends with one trying to escape and one, frustrated, always trying to catch the other. In between are the children, who invariably end up on the side of one parent or the other. Again, at a cost to themselves. Parental discord no matter how subtle always affects children. They feel caught in some way by it. It is in the nature of things that children pick up the imponderables in their parents' lives, lived and unlived. Children unconsciously absorb and take on not only their parents' individual stories, but also that of their relationship.

Eileen was affected in a particular way. She unconsciously took on the wounded part of her mother. Acutely aware of her mother's unhappiness and lack of fulfilment in love, she followed a pattern of falling for a man who was not emotionally available to her. Her soul pulled her to Robert because it wanted to be healed. In this relationship, the whole complicated bundle of her soul wound unravelled itself. She sought to be loved and yet love eluded her.

After the initial romantic and passionate courtship, and increasingly as the children began to arrive, the relationship soured. Robert pulled away as she reached for him. Resentment grew and recriminations followed each disappointment. Each pregnancy exacerbated things in the sense that it loosened a deeper insecurity in Eileen and a fear in Robert. As the marriage progressed, the unfinished business of their respective pasts emerged. New characters appeared. Eileen, forgetting the lightness of being of her love affair with her husband, turned from young woman in love to wounded wife/rejected lover. Robert changed from a charming cool guy to a Peter Pan trying to escape the clutches of what he now saw as a nagging wife. He began to experience her emotional demands on him as smothering, and perhaps suffering from a lack of inner strength that would enable him to stand his ground, he sought to escape. He socialised to excess and he drank.

For many, the consumption of alcohol particularly in times of stress signifies an escape from the pain of living. Alcohol is often referred to as 'spirit'. Psychologically speaking, the sym-

bolism of the word 'spirit' is important. The effects of con-
suming alcohol can give you the illusion of having wings so
that you can escape the restrictions and limitations of your
life. Robert felt limited by his marriage because he had not yet
dealt with the ties that bound him to his mother, and which
dragged him back to childhood. The flight into spirit takes you
away from matter, from the trapping 'mother'. For so often,
the Peter Pan who does not want to grow up will turn his wife
into his mother. Fortunately for Robert, he could drink. Alcohol
did not spell danger for him in the way that it did for his wife.
Drinking and socialising were just one of the ways Robert took
to escape from what he experienced as the 'noose' of marriage, children and responsibilities.

For Eileen, Robert then became the elusive lover and the
absent father. He became the man she longed for but could
not have. The more she wanted from him, the more he edged
away. Desperate for his love, she lost all perspective. They
both did. Things between them got much worse during her
pregnancies. She would become introverted, more involved
with the baby growing inside her. For Robert this stirred up
ghosts; the ghost of his mother who was not there enough for
him when he was a child. Jealous of the attention his wife
seemed to give to her unborn baby, and feeling no connection
with it, he focussed his attentions outside the marriage.

SOUL CONNECTIONS

Eileen and Robert's story is not so unusual. It is a story
of love, fear and disillusionment. A sad story, which I feel,
illustrates what can happen when we get lost in the intricate
tapestry of our family histories. As I wrote earlier in the book
the soul's journey does not end in one lifetime. Life is a continuum, and our soul's existence may span many embodiments. We choose our embodiments in line with our spiritual
challenges. We are born into and inherit our chosen family's
history and the myths of that time. This we call our personal
and archetypal heritage. Each child is born with the contours
of its life already present in potential. This means that we are
born with, and carry memories of both our ancestry and our
future destiny. Our archetypal heritage and our soul's choices
will inform how we go on to live our lives. Our destiny pulls at

us so that, once incarnated, it remembers what our soul needs are, although at a conscious level we will have forgotten.

The soul incarnates into several human lifetimes in order to learn the lessons it needs in order to grow. We may have chosen to come into this embodiment to deal with such things as loss and separation for example. Or to experience the great pull between freedom and belonging that complicates our lives in relationship. Our life is so arranged that such experiences are presented to us as challenges. We will draw into our lives certain people and experiences so that our soul can learn the lessons it has agreed to learn. We do this quite unconsciously because our soul needs are not always apparent to us. At a personality level we flee from pain and so we may find it hard to face the lessons and challenges that life lays before us.

MEN, WOMEN AND CHILDBIRTH

Experiences such as pregnancy and the birth of a child bring many of these hidden challenges to the surface. Having a baby may stir up a huge amount of unresolved conflicts and emotions. In a relationship, no matter how much the baby is planned and welcomed, the new arrival disturbs the equilibrium of the couple. It changes the status quo. If the foundations of a relationship are shaky, then the birth of a child may exacerbate the situation. However, like other challenging situations in life, it may offer an opportunity for growth.

Individually, the mother and the father may have to battle with their own demons, since the birth of a child will tend to dredge up quite different emotions from their respective pasts. For both parents, but more especially for the mother, pregnancy and childbirth may stir up memories and feelings of her childhood. Usually, these are unconscious feelings. They nonetheless become apparent as they are given expression in strong emotions and tensions between the couple.

The young mother may be battling with all sorts of difficult and conflicting feelings, which she may not feel she can share with her partner because she imagines he will not understood them. The father may be engaged in his own inner battles and be either unwilling or unable to voice his feelings. Anxious to keep up appearances, he will often be in denial of anything that he cannot control. His feelings, especially if they are conflicting, may frighten and confuse him. Furthermore he may be preoccupied with what the responsibilities of having a child brings up for him. If communication is not good between the couple, then each will get locked in their own prison of silence. Often, it is men who find it harder to talk about their feelings and this being so, they may not be emotionally available to help their partner or support them at a time when they need it most. Robert for example, could not do it for Eileen.

Traditionally, a man and a woman came together for the purposes of mating and having children. To create a family is a basic archetypal call to which many of us answer. The call of nature is very strong and tugs at most men and women at some stage in their lives. However, in our time of change and the questioning of traditional values, it is not uncommon for relationships to flounder under the strain of parenthood. Instead of bringing a couple together, the birth of children can draw them apart.

Marriages and relationships are breaking up now, as they never were before. And families are becoming fractured with increasing frequency, so that there are a great many children who suffer the loss of one or other parent and the challenges of a 'broken home' or of living with separated parents. This fact creates a need to examine the psychological outcome of such experiences in childhood. The stability of a sound family in which both mother and father are present is not something that can be taken for granted any longer. Children today have different challenges to face, but the formative impact of infancy and childhood has not changed. Since my work is concerned with how children come into the world, I feel there is a need to look more closely at the psychological dynamics of the relationship between men and women. This is one of the reasons I wanted to write this book.

A man and a woman will almost certainly enter partnership and parenthood with varying expectations and fantasies of each other and of their union. Often their expectations differ and they can be mutually disillusioned by the reality of their partnership. Each will bring to their union and to the birth of their children different needs and desires, also different challenges. How each partner meets or fails to meet these challenges will shape both their individual destinies and those of the family they have created together. Psychologically, becoming parents will pull at the unfinished work of their souls and unravel the complicated bundle of their unlived lives. Becoming a parent will inevitably bring up the past, particularly childhood.

DISEMBODIED CONNECTIONS

Women often want more from men. Pregnant women need the committed presence of their partners and the fathers of their children. The reality is that there are a great many factors both collectively and personally, which can make that commitment difficult. Men's archetypal heritage has something to do with a lesser drive to connect emotionally I think. This is especially highlighted in the process of childbirth. Unlike the woman who grows the baby inside her and therefore knows that her child is from her, the father has no such experience. Once a child is conceived, the father can decide to flee from the experience of becoming a father in a way that the mother cannot. On an archetypal level, women are drawn into the experience through their biology. Pregnancy and childbirth serve as initiations into the 'blood' mysteries of the feminine. This helps women to incarnate, or to become embodied. It helps us be more grounded in our physical bodies and in our feelings. Most men today have no access to active initiations, and therefore, in my view, can find it harder to incarnate or to become embodied. There is no comparable experience to pregnancy and childbirth that could serve as an initiation for men. It is difficult for fathers to feel overly connected with the powerful archetypal process of birth, since up to that point the child grows inside the mother. By nature, men are excluded from the experience of pregnancy.

Collectively, there are difficulties also. Quite apart from the difficulties we might have in shaking off a negative and now redundant patriarchy in Western culture, the current climate of repressed feminine consciousness, where feelings must be controlled, makes it difficult to be fully embodied. Western culture with its focus on the rational thinking function whereby we must 'act' rather than 'be' means that the soul and intuitive feeling function is either denied or not taken seriously. This has resulted in a great many psychological problems. It has resulted in a collective loss of soul where men as well as women feel they are missing something.

Denial of the feeling and intuitive functions causes the heart to be torn out of man. Sustaining intimacy in such circumstances is difficult for many people. Some men cannot maintain relationships with women because they fear intimacy. They fear their own vulnerability. This fear and reluctance to open up means that many men avoid close or intimate relationships as much as possible. If they become fathers they may then have difficulty relating emotionally to their children. They become remote figures, perhaps awed and respected, perhaps not, but always just out of reach. Their children then develop a father hunger as they yearn for the close relationship with their fathers that they need in order to develop into secure adults.

DIVIDED HEART

One of the most insidious developments of modern life has been the separation of mind from body. By this I mean that feelings and the senses have come to be associated with the feminine in general and women in particular, while the mind, thought and spirit, are associated with the masculine world. This kind of thinking encourages sex without love and tears the heart out of both men and women. It causes a separation between the masculine and feminine, so that men have come to believe that to be a man one should divorce oneself successfully from one's feelings. It is sad to say that often in Western culture being a man means not expressing emotion and so masculinity is often defined in negative terms: not to cry, not to speak your feelings and so on. If a man is sensitive and blessed with a tender heart, then he fears this weakness in himself as it means he is identifying with women whereas he ought to be tough.

This divide has serious consequences for both men and women. It means that many of us fear love and emotional commitment. For men it often means that they develop a fear of their bodies and bodily needs. Sex becomes divorced from love and the man cannot reach his heart for he has amputated it in the mistaken belief that this makes him more of a man. Guy Corneau, Jungian analyst and author of 'Absent Father Lost Sons', expresses it thus 'It is not that men have no sensitivity; it is rather that they are forbidden to express it if they want to be considered men by other men. In this sense, becoming a man requires cutting oneself off successfully from both the heart and body. In fact one is all the more a man if he manages this amputation without crying or complaining'.

STONE MOTHER CULTURE

Another factor making it difficult to be truly embodied or to 'be there' is the modern medicalisation of childbirth. This modern way of birth has disempowered women by alienating them from their own natures. I explored this in great detail in *Songs from the Womb*. However, it is worth reiterating in this chapter about fathers, and the need for fathers to 'be there'.

Embodiment and relatedness are vitally important in childbirth, an experience of powerful archetypal proportions. If we are not fully in our bodies then we will have trouble birthing and nurturing our babies. And they in turn will have trouble incarnating. This is because parents humanise the archetype of the masculine and the feminine for their children. This means that a child's parents *make real* that child's idea of what male and female is, as well as their expectation of being parented. A girl child needs to identify with her mother to gain access to her femininity, to clothe her bones and draw her female soul into the world. A boy child needs his father in order to fully incarnate as a man. The more remote or absent the child's connection with his parents, the more the child will be influenced by the archetypal mother and father and the more difficult it will be for him to incarnate his own soul.

Jean Shinoda-Bolen, Jungian analyst and author, writes about the mother archetype in many of her books. She describes the four faces of the Great Mother as 'The life-giving, Nurturing Mother and her opposite, the Death Mother; the Ecstatic or Dancing Mother and her opposite, the Stone Mother'. Using the metaphor of the myth of Demeter and Persephone, Bolen explains that when the Nurturing Mother and the Dancing Mother are not present, an emotional wasteland results;

' In Greek mythology, Demeter, Goddess of the Grain, the most giving and bountiful of the Deities, who represented the Mother Goddess at a time when patriarchal religions were becoming predominant, became the Death Mother when she refused to let anything on earth grow and would have allowed hundreds to die of famine.'[1] Her heart and compassion had turned to stone. She had become the 'Stone Mother'.

The theme of the Stone Mother can be witnessed today. It exists somewhere in general consciousness and is given expression every time a mother experiences psychological pain relating to her birth experience and that pain is not acknowledged. It can be witnessed every time a baby is born without due regard to the manner in which he is born. It exists inside us every time we close our hearts and shut the door on our feelings.

When I worked as a prenatal teacher, I saw women struggling to regain the positive or Nurturing Mother and to heal the mother wound during the months of preparation leading up to the birth. Very often, I saw them robbed of whatever they had gained, and I saw them deprived of life-sustaining nourishment. Women were left to labour in a sterile, technological and unfeeling environment. The mother embodied in the institution of medicalised childbirth is often a negative mother, a Stone Mother. She is a Stone Mother because her insistent emphasis on the physical aspect of childbirth at the expense of the spiritual means that many women and their babies have unfulfilling and sometimes very traumatic experiences.

Thinking about what it can be like for women having babies in the current medicalised childbirth culture, I am reminded of the words of TS Eliot:

'There is no water but only rock
Rock and no water and the sandy road
The road winding above among the mountains
Which are mountains of rock without water'.
(TS ELIOT The Wasteland)

Water is life, and here it symbolises the feeling function. Without water and without feeling, people die. We know this. Paediatricians and psychiatrists such as John Bowlby back in the last century found that babies die if they are not loved. He studied babies and children in nurseries, hospitals and orphanages; institutionalised children. Babies and children separated from their mothers suffered a great deal. Though physically cared for, some of these infants pined, as though somehow they had lost the will to live. Some actually physically died from emotional neglect. These babies suffered from an obscure disease called 'failure to thrive', which really means collapsing from lack of love.

NO PLACE TO GO

Men also suffer at the hands of a Stone Mother culture. In some respects they suffer even more because they have no place to go. Many men have retreated to a dry place where there is no water. No feeling. A client of mine used to say that he felt 'hollow' and dry inside. He compared himself to TS Eliot's Hollow Men,

'We are the hollow men
We are the stuffed men
Leaning together
Headpiece filled with straw.'

In order to survive in the outside world, many men have to firmly close the door on their hearts. They have to be able to control their feelings and deny over and over again their inner truths. They get so used to doing this that many have forgotten how to love. Lost in the scramble to achieve in terms of material and economic success, they forget who they really are and what is important. Their own emotional needs are neglected. Unlike women who are 'permitted' to cry and show their feelings, men find this shameful. And so the hurt or distressed man will hold onto his heart pain until sometimes it kills him. Unable to relate intimately to their partners and their children, these men remain locked in a prison of loneliness and isolation. Small wonder then they often cannot 'be there' for their partners in childbirth.

SHADOWLANDS

One must nevertheless acknowledge that modern birthing technology has its place. Many of us, myself included, might not be alive were it not for the life-saving practices of modern medicine. We will never fully eradicate the need for caesarean sections in childbirth for example. And for those who cannot by their own natural means conceive a child, medical technology can offer them that opportunity. But is there a cost? Modern technology offers us much of what we desire but it can also at the same time deprive us of certain, some would even say, vital life experiences. Loss and the ability to mourn not only the death of a loved one but also an unfulfilled dream or wish are experiences that one can do without, you might think. They are nonetheless necessary for our evolution and growth. I believe life experiences, some of which are painful, are offered to us as a way of adding an extra dimension to our lives. They are challenges that enable us to dig deep into our hearts to find inner resources, which once we discover them, remain with us, forever. In the cold light of our modern sanitised technological world, pain and the transformative power of profound life experiences are lost. The dark side of nature is relegated to shadow. Pain loses its meaning and its power to heal us.

Living in a sanitised world can make us intolerant of the shadowlands of our human souls where doubt, uncertainty, grief and a multitude of other emotions remain repressed for as long as we ignore them. Why, in an age of material 'plenty' are so many seeking help in counselling, therapy, New Age healing methods and spirituality? Perhaps it is because pain has lost its meaning. Pain generally does have a meaning and part of its purpose is to draw attention to whatever requires healing in the individual. An integral part of my job as a therapist is to help my clients give meaning to their painful experiences so that they can integrate them into their lives. We recover soul by integrating shadow. It is shadow that gives us depth and when we recover shadow we become embodied. We incarnate, as it were.

A loss of soul in general consciousness is something that has been acknowledged by many, particularly in the western world. 'Richer in wealth, poorer in spirit.' leads the front page of a national Irish newspaper. 'Ireland is thriving', so we are told. 'Our economy is second only to that of Luxembourg. We ought to be a happy and fulfilled nation brimming with goodwill and joie de vivre'. Not so. It appears that health and wealth are not synonymous. Most of us know this of course, but we are nonetheless shocked when we read statements such as: 'we continue to experience the biggest growth in male suicides of any country in Europe. It is startling', the article continues 'that so many young people should feel so alienated from society and so devoid of hope that their only option is self-destruction. This is even more surprising since our increasing suicide rate is happening at a time when psychiatric illness was never more easily treated and when openness about suicide and emotional problems was never so great'.

These sentiments can be shared by any developed nation in the Western world. On the other side of the Atlantic children barely out of infancy are killing each other with guns, something that, horrifyingly, the American public has come to accept as not uncommon. The relative frequency of these appalling incidents may bring us to wonder whether we are now witnessing the death of childhood. How has this happened? Perhaps it has something to do with the way we now communicate with each other. With easier access to computers generally, communication is becoming increasingly electronic. Instead of going out to play in the street with their friends, many children spend days glued to their monitors, chatting to unknown and unseen electronic 'mates'.

Do these disembodied connections mean we are losing the art of relating to real people? Are we becoming alienated from our human, genuine selves? Perhaps these children are expressing something of that. One of the young Arkansas killers is reported to have said that he wanted to kill all the girls who had broken up with him. That a 13-year-old boy already had a string of exgirlfriends speaks volumes. The painful irony of course is that this young boy killed for love. If you are desperate for love but lack the emotional vocabulary to handle it, then it is easy to 'kill the thing you love'.

Jung was right when he wrote, over half a century ago now, that man had lost his soul. Modern living has given rise to a sense of loss, which we feel as a cry from the soul. Emotional isolation and loneliness appear to be on the increase as we give birth to our fears about truly entering the human race. Not accepting our true nature with its dark as well as its light side means that we are not in balance. We are not complete.

WOUNDED FATHERS

Men suffer from soul loss in a very particular way. When a man loses his connection with his *anima* he loses the ability to relate. Jung used the term *anima* to describe the feminine aspect in men, the inner image of woman. The anima like its counterpoint in women, the animus is a soul image. As I already stated, it is an archetypal force and is not gender related in the sense that all men and women have masculine and feminine energies. When a man loses his connection to his anima it means that his feminine energy is wounded. This feminine energy is the very thing he needs to form a bridge, not only from himself to others, but also from his internal to his external world. When he loses touch with the ability to feel and identify his feelings, his anima is imprisoned in shadow, while he becomes increasingly identified with his *persona*.

As I said previously, I believe that the turning upside down of traditional roles has gradually and subtly eroded the confidence of many men to be lovers to their women and fathers to their children. As a result of the huge increase in marriage break-ups and a separate but related rise in the numbers of single parent families, fathers often become marginalised and disempowered. Stripped of their material possessions, their homes and sometimes even their children, many broken fathers suffer in silence.

Because society is structured in such a way as to make it much harder for men to admit defeat and hurt, many of them hide behind a wall of denial of their true needs, and fill up their lives in any way they can. Pubs, race meetings, sports clubs are full of broken men, who valiantly soldier on in a world that for them has become devoid of love. Settling for the lowlands of comfort and complacency and sex without emotional involvement, the hurt man may gradually close down his own need for love. When a hurt man who has put a skin around his heart does meet a woman who wants to love him, often he does not know how to respond, and so he loses her.

CHIRON THE WOUNDED HEALER

We have seen how certain aspects of modern living inhibit our ability or willingness to 'be there', to be embodied, and to be fully present. And yet if we are to heal our soul loss, we must recover what we have lost. Perhaps we can look to mythology to find some answers to our struggle. Jungian psychology frequently uses myth as a way of telling a story. Mythological characters and their stories symbolise for us the journey of the human soul with its many trials and tribulations. 'Myths are a way of telling a story that has a universal appeal. It has been defined as something that never was but always is. There is something about myth that transcends race and culture and touches what is essentially human in each of us'[2].

To be fully and truly embodied means to accept, inhabit and live our humanity in full. Like Chiron, the wounded healer in Greek mythology, it means accepting our mortality. For, it is only by accepting and fully embracing our mortality and our pain that we can ultimately touch the hand of God and free Prometheus, our creative spirit. The myth of Chiron symbolises for us what happens when we are wounded in our 'feeling' side and therefore disconnected at some profound level from ourselves.

As you may recall, Chiron, who was half man half horse (a centaur), was wounded in the thigh, in his horse or 'animal' side. A progeny of the Greek God Zeus, he was born as a result of his father's mating with a nymph who changed herself into a mare to escape his attentions. Abandoned at birth, he was reared by the God Apollo and was skilled in the arts but neglected in his instinctual nature. He became a gifted healer. Nothing he did however could heal him of his wound. Since he was a God he could not 'die', and so his pain continued. He had to trade his immortality and make a bargain with Zeus to release Prometheus in order to 'die' and be restored to health. Prometheus was the Titan who was chained to a rock for attempting to steal fire from the Gods. He represents the creative spirit of man. The symbolism of the myth is clear. In other words, Chiron had to embrace his humanity, his wounds and his 'animal' instinctual side, in order to heal himself. While he was not fully 'embodied' this could not happen.

From this myth we learn that in order to become embodied we must embrace our mortality, our humanness. Chiron's 'death' symbolises in psychological terms, the death of the ego. The willingness to let go and move on. In practical terms this means accepting our wounds. It means connecting with our inner selves, our feelings. Since nowadays our feelings are often relegated to shadow, it means recovering our *shadow*.

RECOVERING SHADOW

As stated earlier, the *shadow* is a term used in Jungian psychology to describe all that we repress and more. It comprises both the contents of our personal unconscious and the collective unconscious. Our shadows not only comprise what we would perceive as our negative aspects, but also our potentialities. What we could be, or become - qualities we have not as yet activated. Recovering the shadow is not always easy or pleasant. It involves suffering and the willingness to suffer. It involves accepting the darker or less pleasant side of our personality. It also involves the willingness to let go of old ego patterns that may have served us once, but are now no longer appropriate. It means having the courage to change.

As we have seen, loss of soul happens when there is a division between body and mind. The soul is what unites the two aspects of our human nature so that we are, therefore, complete and whole. I like to use the image of the cross, an ancient symbol, to remind us of the union of earth/body and spirit/mind. The vertical line depicts unearthed spirituality and the horizontal line de-spirited earth. They meet together in the middle, i.e. the heart. It is in the heart that man connects with both spirit and matter. The wisdom of the heart is where soul resides. Reclaiming soul makes us whole.

Accepting our humanness is part of this. There is always pain to be suffered as part of the human condition. We must be willing to suffer because suffering and struggle helps us grow. Pain can make us leave however. It can make us escape so that part of us is not at home. Similarly, when confronted with birth and death, with fundamental life events, we can find difficulty staying with the process as it unfolds. These experiences take us to the edge of life. Birth and death take us to deep places where we are confronted with our own limitations and our mortality. Staying when it gets tough is not easy. When something frightens us we often run away or want to run away. Or we take refuge; we dull our senses when something is too painful to be borne.

In the case of childbirth, it may be drugs or unnecessary medicalisation, some of which are used, it must be said, in the service of alleviating the anxiety of the birth attendants rather than that of the mother! Fear and the suspicion of nature; fear of the human condition; fear of pain cause birth and death to become shrouded in a cloud of anaesthesia as well as sometimes violent and invasive practices which rob us of soul. The sanctity of the whole experience is then lost to us.

At the dawn of the twenty first century we are living in a time of great change, a liminal time where what we know is falling apart and no longer true, and what is to come is not yet formed. It is a time of upheaval. 'Liminal' means threshold. It means to be betwixt and between. We are living now in an age where technology is able to give us almost anything we desire in a material sense. Yet at the same time, the huge growth of mind/body/spirit or positive living consciousness is witness to our dissatisfaction. A part of us realises that to go on the way we are going means death of a sort. Our present way of living is costing us too much. Despite our 'advanced' technology we are hungry. Or rather our soul is hungry. Starved of soul food we rush to our nearest mind/body/spirit bookstore, Reiki practitioner or spiritual healer to be healed from a soul wound we are not able to identify.

We are between two places, one of lack and one of plenty. Here in Ireland we are enjoying one of the fastest growing economies in Western Europe. We also have dark shadows- an increasing crime rate and an escalating suicide rate particularly amongst young men. In the Western world, natural childbirth has almost been made redundant by large-scale technological advancements whereby caesarean sections have become a matter of choice of birth, and babies have become commodities. They are now being technologically created to meet consumer demand. Sperm and egg as well as wombs have become objects detached from their human homes. Human beings are being fabricated in laboratories and then implanted in wombs that have become mere growing mediums. Women are leasing their wombs to the highest bidders.

Mothers are having their son's babies, and there is talk of human cloning as well as the possibility of creating babies without the use of sperm. Having a baby is, paradoxically, still the same as it has ever been and yet aspects of the process have changed irrevocably and beyond recognition. Something is missing.

BEING THERE

Eileen wanted Robert to 'be there'. She wanted something solid yet intangible from him. Childbirth is a woman's domain, but behind her lives her man. He is her provider and supporter. By doing so, he leaves her free to do her job. Father's presence and his role in childbirth needs to be found and acknowledged. It needs to be recognised that there is a need for the father on many levels, not just the physical and economical. By that I mean that he needs to be acknowledged not only as provider and breadwinner as well as supportive partner, but also as an essential presence for both the new baby and its mother.

On a soul level, the child needs to feel welcomed by both his mother and his father, for he has chosen these as his parents. On a personality level, a father's psychological presence is very significant for the growth and development of his child. In normal circumstances, a pregnant woman needs the solid and firm commitment of the father of her child at all times, most especially so around the time of the birth. Pregnancy is a time when a woman loosens her boundaries and ties with the external world. In order to be free to bond with her unborn child and embrace the whole powerful process, she needs to know that her partner is dealing with the practical side of their daily life.

Because of the way modern society has evolved, there is often scant recognition of the way in which the male female balance needs to shift during pregnancy. With the pressures of modern living, a pregnant woman is often expected to hold down a job as well as running the home. The internal hormonal shifts responsible for the changes within her are not generally honoured. For economic reasons, for example, she may be obliged to work outside the home. As a result she may feel pulled between the external world and the internal world that she inhabits with her child. This conflict tends to become more pronounced according as her pregnancy advances and greater emotional and physical demands are placed on her. If she does not have a partner who is both physically and emotionally supportive she will feel the strain. Studies indicate that pregnant women, who are well supported emotionally, go on to have easier and less troublesome births and better relationships with their children.

An expectant mother goes through enormous changes as a result of her pregnancy and the effects of great hormonal shifts in her body. Just as her body is changing, so is her soul. We saw this with Cifre in the first chapter. Pregnant women become emotionally labile. It is part of being pregnant. Rocking in this wind of change, in pregnancy we seek structure and safety. We need it in order to feel safe enough to let go and to run with the forces of nature inside us. A strong male presence can help us feel grounded. We naturally want to lean on our husbands or partners. We need them to 'be there' for us.

I have worked with a great many couples during childbirth and I myself have had three children. I know from my own experience how profoundly important it is for a woman to feel loved when she is pregnant. We all need love, but a pregnant woman needs love of a very particular kind. She has an increased need to feel emotionally supported. She needs to be released from whatever she holds emotionally for her partner in order to be free to nurture her growing child. During pregnancy there is a natural tendency towards introversion. A woman gradually becomes less concerned with external events and is instead drawn into the unconscious and the world of her unborn child. If she is open to it, a pregnant woman may go through a transformation that is not merely physical. She will be open to change and growth and will have access to the spiritual in a way not possible previously. If she accepts the challenge to change, then pregnancy and the birth of her child will facilitate her transformative process.

For the expectant father the process is quite different. He may be very affected by the thought of becoming a father, but because he is not experiencing the powerful physical changes that his partner is experiencing, he may feel more remote from the process. At this stage, his child and the fact that he is to become a father are only thoughts. It may be difficult for him to feel connected to his child and even his partner. He might feel that he has lost her to the whole experience of pregnancy and the impending birth of their child. Many men tell me they felt excluded from the process of becoming a parent. Their baby is growing inside their partner and they are unsure how they can help or be part of the unborn baby's life.

As well as that, an 'expectant' father will have to deal with what exactly becoming a father means to him. It may require a deeper level of commitment than perhaps he has ever felt before. It may mean he will have two or more people totally dependent on him and for whom he must provide. Depending on how commitment and responsibility sits with him, he will experience various reactions. If he is afraid of failure for example, no matter how unconscious that fear might be he might react to the news of impending fatherhood with trepidation. Will he be able to provide? Will he earn enough money? What about his partner? She was his lover. When she becomes a mother, will he lose her? Will she forget about him? If he harbours a latent insecurity then it may loosen itself at this time.

DESPERADOS

It is easy to become a desperado, unable to come off the fence or make a commitment to life. Emotional alienation, violence, soul hunger, loss of spirit- they all indicate that we have lost our way, that in some way we fear full embodiment. It is hard for us to 'be there'. The prevailing culture virtually ostracises feelings and the intuitive voices of the soul, making it difficult for relationships and for parenthood. This means that our children have to find their way alone. The more we retreat from our souls and our inner world, the more we are cut off from our feelings, and the harder it is for our children to come into the world in a fully embodied way. In a time of no heart we need to be there more than ever, if we are to help our children incarnate as soulful human beings.

Notes

1.   J. Shinoda-Bolen, *Crossing to Avalon*, HarperCollins, (1994), p.177
2.   M. Deane, referenced in *Changing Fathers* ed. Mc Keown, K. (1998) p.53

CHAPTER NINE

LOVE IN A TIME OF LOSS

Keep love in your heart. A life without it is like a sunless gar-
den when the flowers are dead. The consciousness of loving
and being loved bring a warmth and richness to life that noth-
ing else can bring.

(Oscar Wilde, In Conversation)

Laced throughout the chapters of this book has been the loss of soul that we are all suffering from in one way or the other. From the absent father, to the difficulties of relating emotionally and maintaining healthy family relationships, it is obvious that modern living has given rise to a need to reclaim our souls. Restoring our ability to love is the key to healing our soul wounds.

Love is an ideal to which all human beings aspire. It is said that love is the prime motivator of all human action. Love inspires us, challenges us and moves us. It is also said that there are but two human emotions love and fear. Fear is the opposite of love. Because the human condition and our life experience make it difficult for us to trust and maintain the love ideal in practice, we often succumb to fear and this blocks our ability to love and be loved. We cease to trust. When we make life choices that are motivated by fear it is because we have lost touch with our essence, our divine natures. At those times our light and our ability to love and to trust become opaque and we forget who we really are. As the pages of this book bear out, we are all born with the capacity to love and be loved. From a spiritual perspective, we are souls clothed in human form and our essence is divine. However, faced with the challenges and the hardships that life offers us, we often falter and lose our way. We lose touch with our ideals. We become discouraged. Our resultant soul loss leads us some-times to become physically and mentally sick.

One of the ways to recover soul in our lives is to take a spiritual and sometimes philosophical approach to our difficulties. Accepting that life has thrown particular challenges at us, such as the breakdown of love and marriage, in order to help us to grow, can aid our pain and hasten our recovery. When we take this approach we cease to be victims of life and we empower ourselves. In the next chapter I write about recovering the inner king who represents our strength and our ability to fight for our beliefs and integrity. Although this book is primarily about honouring and recovering fathers and the masculine principle, inner harmony and completion cannot happen without incorporating the feminine principle. In this chapter I write about recovering another aspect of our souls, our inner feminine, which symbolically represents our ability to feel, to love and to suffer. We need both in order to be at peace and to experience inner and outer harmony.

THE HEART THAT LOVES IS ALWAYS YOUNG

Since it is the nature of ideals to both inspire us and disappoint us, during the course of our lives, our hearts are often broken. Although we aspire to love and be loved, most of us at some stage in our lives face the death of love in a relationship or a marriage. This is not necessarily a bad thing. In many ways, suffering the death of the heart helps us grow. It was Oscar Wilde who said that hearts are meant to be broken. I understand this. We have to die in order to be born again. In order to grow we have to let go of what we were in the past. Like a plant, we have to shed the dead leaves of our past to make room for new buds to sprout. If we don't shed what is no longer useful to our growth and progress, then we stifle and prevent further growth. This is the essence of God, life and death. It is the cycle of life, one which we are all destined to experience. It is also said that 'the heart that loves is always young'. When we love, we live. When we have suffered the death of love in a relationship however, we feel pain, and we vow never to fall in love again. When we do, we feel life and we grow. A heart that loves is constantly renewing itself.

It is interesting to note that after a traumatic life event such as the loss of a loved one, it is common to have dreams of love. A woman who had lost her husband of thirty years was appalled when a short time later she began to have erotic, sexual dreams. With the death of her husband, and being past middle age, she had thought that that part of her life was over. However, her dreams signified the stirrings of renewed life and suggested that her soul was healing. Sexual relating in dreams symbolises the desire to connect with life, with one's creativity and life force. In a bereaved person these dreams usually signify the beginning of the healing period. The irrepressible push of new life is part of nature. Life always seeks to express itself.

DEATH OF THE HEART

All human beings experience loss during the course of their lives. Every time we suffer such a loss we experience a 'death of the heart' in some form or another. With the great increase in marital breakdown, we are fast approaching a time when everyone will have experienced the death of the heart in the severing of a major intimate relationship. Although, as previously said, the experience of loss is often a catalyst to growth, I believe that there is cause for concern about the emotional wellbeing of modern man. At the beginning of a new Millennium, when many people, young men in particular, feel so alienated from life that they actually resort to suicide, we must accept that something has gone wrong. There is a great heart wound in general consciousness; many men and women are hurt emotionally. Many men are in the desert. Many women are also in the desert. We are there perhaps because those men we love cannot relate to us, or us to them. We are in the desert because somewhere, somehow, the art of truly relating to each other has been lost. And although our hearts are still beating, they are beating to a different tune. A less open tune, a more muted tune laced with tentative hope and incipient loneliness.

True emotional and physical intimacy involves trust and the ability to open up to the other. So many of us, who have had our trust betrayed in the past, find it hard to relate on an intimate level and we remain isolated in a protective shell. In the grip of fear, we assume all sorts of veneers and behaviour patterns, which are designed to protect us but which in reality, actually isolate us not only from others but also from ourselves. Emotional and sexual celibacy can be positive life choices for those who make them, but very often they are imposed on us because of our own fears of relating to other human beings. Too many of us are cut off from our true feelings and from the voices of our souls. And so we find ourselves living in an emotional wasteland.

I have written earlier about the emotional wasteland into which babies are born when modern medical birthing practice results in a loss of soul in both mother and child. If the cultural and emotional climate into which we are born is not conducive to opening up and flowing with our Divine natures then we become disillusioned, gradually closing down our heart centres. By doing so, we encounter a great many difficulties because, in effect, we are blocking our life force, our true essence. When we form relationships with our heart centres closed, and then we are operating from lower energy centres, our relationships will be based less on a love ideal and more on such things such as sex, money, emotional and material security or power. These relationships may be functional but, ultimately, they will not make us happy and, as a result, they will often fail.

As I wrote earlier, loving and being loved are ideals that all human beings aspire to. To be in love and to love are archetypal forces. They are one of the strongest, if not the strongest, motivators of human existence. Because of the cultural and emotional climate that we have created in the West men in particular now find it hard to relate intimately. And this leaves women who wish to relate in this way with both a hunger and emptiness. Whether it is because, like the book says, 'women are from Venus and men are from Mars' or simply because of the way we have evolved as human beings, men often have no one and nowhere to turn to when they are hurt. They often cannot talk about what they are feeling. It is different for us. Women seem to have a greater ability to relate on an intimate level. We talk about affairs of the heart with relative ease. We do not feel we are losing face if we bare our souls and open our hearts. We network and we help each other on an emotional level. We are more grounded in the art of expressing feelings. If we are having difficulties in a relationship and we are in pain we will call our women friends and talk or cry into the phone. Men rarely do this.

As I write this I have just learnt of the death by suicide of yet another young man. A young man of barely eighteen years old, a contemporary of my son and daughter, who took his own life because he could not stand the pain he was suffering as a result of the break-up of a love relationship. Such news is both shocking and dreadfully sad. In my view, it is a terrible indictment of modern living that a young person feels they have no option but to put an end to their own lives. In essence, this is about the deep alienation or soul loss of modern man. The fact that significantly more men than women commit suicide points to the increased estrangement of men who are unable to find a place of solace when they are hurting or in despair. The life of that young boy might have been saved if he could have spoken of his pain to someone.

INTO THE DESERT

Life mutilates our ideals horribly, and yet we cannot really live without them. Ideals are designed to inspire us and spur us into action as well as pull us down to earth to face our mortality. When we fall in love and it doesn't work out, our ideal along with our dream of love is smashed. We retreat into the shadows of our disappointment. We may become hard and cynical and decide to close the door on our hearts if we have been hurt many times. Eventually, we may become so cynical we forget that we are spiritual beings of light. We imagine then that love does not exist, and worse, that we do not need it; that it is for the foolish and for the hopeless romantic.

After the break-up of a marriage or a love relationship, our ideals are shattered and many of us retreat to the desert, to a cold place of no heart. The Irish poet Colm O'Connor describes this well.[1]

'...And as men we go unseen and unblessed
as if unwelcome into the intimacies of life
And we turn then
We all turn then and walk into the desert with deep
hunger'.

Of course it is not only men of who suffer this way. I felt moved to write about fathers and sons and lovers and about the death of the heart in both men and women because both in my clinical work and in my personal life I have encountered this desert experience. I have loved and lost many times.

Some years ago, while struggling with the break-up of a relationship I wrote this poem, which I called Golden Boy. This was my name for the love ideal embodied in the man I had loved and lost. It also represented, I saw later, my soul at the time, my creative energy, which I had invested in him.

Borne on Divine wings
The golden boy is swift in motion
Passing this way and that
Hardly leaving a mark so light is he
Those fortunate enough to cross his path
Are sprinkled with the gift of joy
He brings on the wings of his desire

But desire once born to mortals is fatal
For it hurls us headlong into an endless search
Destined only to failure
He, being unattached, can move on
And does not try to harness what is free

I've met you golden boy
We danced together for a while
Your soul and mine held hands
There was magic as we loved
The kind lovers only dream of
A million stars burst into song by night
And a warm golden sun followed us by day

Then, as suddenly as you came,
You disappeared
The stars dimmed their lights
The sun went out of my life
The magic gone
I was left alone

Perhaps I had tried to hold you
For you were my Prince
My sun, my moon, my stars,
Blinded by my desire and

Intoxicated with the magic we created
I was your Princess for a while
And I forgot
I forgot that we are mortals
And that being so, desire would bind us
I wanted the magic to go on forever

I had held you golden boy
And then you were a man
Hard and strong in your desire for the woman in me
I had felt your heartbeat my quiet man
You had held me in your strong arms
And I had touched your wounded heart
And so
You grew frightened I would hold you
And flew away

But it was too late,
For the Gods had seen it too
The time had come
Perhaps too soon for one so young
Still, mortality demands a price
And love does too

Empty after you left I lived in a dark world
With only memories to lighten the bruise in my heart
And the tear in my soul
With bitter tears I called you back
But you were gone and only the wind answered
I grew thin with pain
And when finally I buried you on that still day
I had no life or hope
But a shell I carried wearily along

I had loved him so much I had put everything into him and so, when I lost him, I imagined I had nothing. So many of us do this when we fall in love. We imagine we cannot live without the other person. In essence though, what we have lost is that part of ourselves we saw mirrored in the other, a lost fragment of our soul. Although we cannot see it then, what we are being challenged to do is to find that lost part in ourselves. I suffered as anyone who has lost a lover does.

Initially, I too closed the doors of my heart and dragged myself around as though mortally wounded. I turned inwards. I wrote and my writing helped me. I returned to my soul home and found peace in walking by the sea and immersing myself in nature. In the struggle to regain my sense of myself and heal my heart of this love wound, I grew. I learnt about my own ability to love. In a sense, I found my inner man, my own golden boy. I once read that nothing ever ends without something better beginning. I gained solace from that. Finally, some months later, I was able to write:

> *Then one day*
> *As I walked in the wet land of my tears*
> *The pain in my chest grew too much for my soul to*
> *bear*
> *And I sat down on the damp earth to rest*
> *Fearing death, I covered my heart with my hands*
> *And lowered my head till it rested on the grass*
> *I heard again the beating heart of nature*
> *And then my own*
> *I saw you rise from the earth, a small flame at first*
> *Then your body of clay formed around the golden light*
> *And there you were, my golden boy*
> *But a boy no more*
> *For as I looked you grew into the strong man*
> *I had mated with*
> *You stepped across and lifted me up in the strong arms*
> *I had once known*
> *In a timeless embrace*
> *The circle closed around us and I knew*
> *I knew then that it would never break again.*

SPEAKING FROM THE HEART

There are a number of factors that make relationships between men and women difficult. One of these is a discrepancy in the willingness and ability to speak from the heart. When I asked my partner to speak from the heart, he did not understand what I meant. This was not because he had no heart or no voice, but because he could not use them simultaneously. This is not an exclusively male phenomenon. As children we are often discouraged from expressing our emotions and many families never talk about personal feelings. Many of us grow up repressing our feelings and we then lose the ability to articulate them at all. Those of us who have done inner work, whether as part of our training as therapists or otherwise, will have regained some of what we have lost and we will be able to speak from the heart from time to time. But again, it appears that men prefer to walk out into the desert or crawl into their caves rather than articulate what they feel.

In a great many instances, men find it hard to relate intimately at all because of difficulties in speaking from the heart. If a man cannot articulate his feelings in an intimate relationship, then this leaves not only him but also his partner feeling isolated. Out of frustration, the partner of a man who cannot speak from the heart may push him to do so in order to address difficulties that have arisen in the relationship. This almost never works. As the partner of a man who had great difficulty speaking from the heart, I learnt that the more I forced him to say or do something, the more I pushed him away. Waiting and leaving the space for him to come to me worked. It was a hard lesson, but in essence, relating to this man taught me to accept that men approach things differently. Women who are involved with this type of man need to learn to not only wait but also to read the signals.

Men often demonstrate their feelings through deed and action rather than words. Indeed, a great many men do not articulate their feelings because they may be unable to identify them in the first place. They have got used to disregarding their emotions and treating them like unwanted guests. For some, like James for example, emotions are the cause of great confusion; they are a nuisance and interference in a normal rational way of behaving. A man who is not used to dealing with his feelings will do almost anything to keep them at bay. Of course all he actually succeeds in doing is creating more pain and confusion. From the woman's perspective all her partner is achieving is simply blocking her and preventing their relationship from flowing freely.

Not speaking from the heart creates obvious difficulties in a relationship. Many founder because of it. If prolonged, lack of communication in a relationship will usually lead to its demise. In the gap that opens up between two people experiencing difficulty, misconceptions, misinterpretations, hurt and rejection take their place. The walls that both partners erect to protect themselves from the pain of loving and relating make true communication from the heart impossible. They merely serve to increase the couple's isolation from each other. After a while spent living this way, you begin to forget your true feelings. Longing gets confused with resentment, and anger and love become twisted in a complicated mesh of emotions that are difficult to unravel. You may lose all clarity about whether what you are feeling belongs to you or to your partner. You become all mixed up emotionally.

Men generally are better at cutting off than women. They have the capacity to separate their feelings from their external lives and they can carry on their normal work and life routines regardless of the howling pain inside them. Conversely, for most women, their emotional lives can interface with their external lives. A woman who is suffering pain in her relationship will often feel the need to externalise it by talking to someone. Relating is our way; we want to sort things out. Men on the other hand suppress their feelings and hide in their caves until they feel better. Only then can the matter be resolved. Of course, often it is not resolved since the man often hides away from the conflict and simply hopes that it will go away. When couples seek counselling, it is almost invariably the woman who 'brings' the man to the first session. I often feel that for male partners, talking about or exteriorising the problems in their relationship is very difficult and even shameful.

SEXUAL VULNERABILITY

I believe there is another factor that makes it harder for men to open up, thereby further contributing to psychological or emotional inequality between the sexes. Men today are sexually vulnerable in a way that they were not previously. Ever since feminist principles finally took hold, women have become stronger and have found their voice. They will spell out their needs and expect men to fulfil them. Furthermore, as I wrote earlier, the King is dead. Many of us no longer hold the image of King in our psyches and in our hearts. Instead our minds and hearts house the image of a fallen King. This has implications for how we women relate to men. Since our psychic images inform not just our thoughts but also our behaviour and our feelings, modern women have different expectations of men. We may be more demanding. We expect our needs to be met. Often, they will not be met. When they are not, we feel let down, with the result that we may see these men as failures. A fallen King will inevitably fail us.

One of the outcomes of the sexual revolution is that women no longer have to be coaxed and seduced into making love. Often they will seek men out and will expect to be satisfied sexually. This can put men under pressure. Women are stronger today in a great many ways, and so a man needs to feel very confident and secure in himself in order to feel equal. A strange juxtaposition of roles has occurred. The male female balance is upset. A great many men tell me they feel under pressure to perform, sexually and otherwise. Some buckle under the pressure; others try to escape by avoiding intimacy.

The fear of not measuring up to a woman's needs and expectations is one of the most common emotions I hear expressed by my male clients. This fear of failure can force men out of the relationships arena altogether. There is a lot of shame attached to the Fallen King. Men fear losing face and fear of failure makes them withdraw. Their withdrawal at times of stress increases relationship problems. The more they withdraw in relationships, the more frustrated women get, and the more they seek from their partners. It is like a vicious circle.

I had an interesting discussion with a very wise and serene older man a short time ago, which made me reflect a lot about the tender nature of men's sexual pride and the need in some way to honour the Inner King. As women and as lovers we have tremendous power I believe. It is a subtle kind of power because it is delicate as well as deep, indirect and intangible. It has to do with the ability to pick up information through sense, feeling, and intuition. Armed with this knowledge, we can either destroy or restore a man's sexual pride and his ability as a lover with one or two simple words.

Wounded men in particular are very susceptible to the influence of the Fallen King. If a woman projects such an image onto her partner, and then consistently finds fault with him or criticises him, he may begin to identify with a negative image and so will fail her more and more. Women who are not in touch with their inner feminine natures are more inclined to project the fallen king image onto their partners and to criticise them. When a woman appears demanding and controlling, we say in Jungian psychological language that she is 'animus ridden'. This means that she is taken over by her negative animus.

In the next chapter I will write about the need to recover our own inner king. When we do this, we free our partners from our projections and we have a better chance of achieving and maintaining harmonious relationships. We need to recover the Inner King and the outer King will follow.

WAKING FROZEN LOVERS

There is another common psychological dynamic that is played out between lovers. When love is equated with loss then great fear accompanies it. When a man carries a father wound, his hurt is often greater than his ability to love. Despite the fact that he will have drawn into his life a woman who will challenge him to open his heart, he will often turn away from love. The woman who loves him may experience it thus. She may weep in despair when her love is not returned. She knows he has the potential to love, and she wonders why he cannot do so. When her call receives no answer she despairs.

Waking frozen lovers appeared to be Isabel's destiny. She had experienced it several times in her life. When Isabel loved, she lost herself. She knew about frozen love because her birth wound predisposed her to experience it. It surfaced in her relationships once her heart was touched. When she opened her heart to her lover, Isabel's wound would open to sing it's song again, and a great need would be awakened in her. Craving love from frozen and hurt lovers she would get lost in the storm of her desires. Love would be lost in her attempts to find it. As I have said earlier, it is in the nature of things that what we crave most, we often push away and so love eludes us.

Desperate, Isabel would prize open her wounded heart prematurely. She generally did this by choosing very hurt men as her lovers. These men were destined to disappoint her because more often than not, as with James, their fear of hurt meant they could not return her love, at least overtly. They were unable to express how they felt and she would get frustrated. The more she sought from them the more they pulled away. They needed time to thaw out. Isabel knew this at some level, but invisible strings from her heart seemed to pull her, and she ceased to recognise what she knew to be the truth. The messages from her heart confused her.

A wounded heart is like a crushed flower. It must be allowed to open in its own time, undisturbed, loved from a distance, as the rays of the sun help a plant to grow. Isabel remembered that James had, in his own words, told her this. In the kitchen, that spring afternoon, he had held her and asked her to wait, to let him grow to trust and love her. 'Leave it to me', he had said as he stepped back from the intensity of their relationship. 'It won't always be like this. I won't always have my walls erected around me'. But Isabel found it hard to wait.

What she failed to recognise was that she was a frozen lover herself; that inside her own tender and open heart was a very wounded child who did not know how to love without losing herself entirely. Who feared love above all else. Who was so desperate to find love that she would frequently travel down all sorts of unlikely roads, and in the process, cause herself pain and humiliation. Her ceaseless search for love and validation blinded her to what she already had. It caused her to push away love when it came too close. Isabel pushed James away with the kind of ferocity and tangled pain that is typical of hurt lovers' relationships. She tested and retested him until, exhausted, he fled from her relentless anxiety and her restless soul.

When he fled, she suffered in the resulting emptiness. Then, finding no escape from the ceaseless and intolerable pain inside her, she also fled. She fled to a very small place inside herself. She withdrew from the world. At those times of pain, Isabel's world became too big for her to manage, and she would retreat from everything and everyone. Only the wind and the sounds of the sea could soothe her torn soul and her aching heart.

RECOVERING SOUL: HEALING THE HEART

In order to recover soul we need to heal the heart. This is not easy for it involves having the courage to acknowledge our wounds and suffer them. However, if we do not do so, we are left in the desert. It takes great courage to take up the challenge to heal our soul wounds. In my experience, it appears to be particularly hard for men at this time. As a consequence, it is also difficult for women since it makes maintaining relationships problematic. My work as a therapist means that I have been privileged to see, feel and sense the inside story of a great many wounded men and fathers. My heart goes out to these men. I have been allowed access through the locked gates of hearts frozen with fear. I have been there during the gradual thawing of the heart, the fight for survival, and finally, the recovery of the Inner King.

On a personal level also, I meet many men who have a history of hurt caused by broken marriages and relationships. Indeed, I have been through it myself. After many years of self imposed isolation and inner work, I finally found the courage to begin a relationship with a man who became my lover and partner. We were both casualties of the past. We had both experienced the death of the heart in different ways. Locked in our mutual protective shells, it took time to negotiate the ravaged coastlands of our hearts and begin to trust and open up to each other.

MOURNING THE DEATH OF THE HEART

One of the greatest stumbling blocks to love is failure to deal with loss. The death of the heart must be mourned. If we have suffered the break-up of a marriage or long-term relationship, then we may carry over these losses into the next relationship, particularly if those losses and other losses in our lives remain unresolved. For example, we may carry the corpses of past relationships, with thwarted expectations and unmet needs around in our hearts. We may see our current partners through the lenses of past experiences. Our hearts can be catacombs, incarcerating our former partners and the memories that we retain of those partnerships. We confuse then the present with the past and our new lover assumes the mantle of his predecessors. We lose touch with the here and now as our future is mapped out by our fears.

If we believe that we are unable to sustain healthy relationships then we will project these negative beliefs into the present and literally make it a reality. If we have suffered great loss in love then our fears of loving again will be very great. We will do almost anything to avoid the pain involved in betrayal and loss but unconsciously we will attract it to us through the power of negative energy unless we are willing to overcome our fears. Unshed tears can fill up our heart space so that it becomes a block to loving again. When we release the pain and grief associated with loss, the energy of love can flow freely again.

The nearest symbolic equivalent that comes to mind is of the loss of a child. The loss of a child as a result of miscarriage or abortion or shortly after birth is, I believe, one of the most painful things a woman can experience. It is an embodied loss, by which I mean it is felt not only in the psyche and in the heart, but also deep within the body itself. In addition, the loss of a child is always the loss of unfulfilled life and this adds to its impact. To the trauma of loss is added the pain of losing 'what might have been', the loss of potential in all its manifestations. Many broken relationships take on that quality of loss, since often one or other partner does not want the relationship to end. If it has come to a timely end and both partners are agreed on that, then the parting although painful, will not have the same impact as an unresolved ending.

I lost two babies early on in pregnancy and I found both experiences very traumatic. It took me a long time to mourn their loss and to move on. In a strange sort of way, losing them blocked me from moving on even though after some time I did have other children. In common with most women who have lost babies, giving birth to other children subsequently healed the pain of my loss to some extent, but it never replaced them in my heart. We always wonder what the child would have been like. As is the case with most mothers, I remember their birth dates and what age they would have been had they lived.

Some four years after losing my last child in pregnancy and well after my marriage had broken up, I experienced the premature ending of a relationship. It was a brief love affair that ended abruptly just as it was developing. To me it felt like a terrible loss quite similar to a miscarriage or an abortion. What was most difficult for me yet again, was the loss of 'what might have been', the potential of a love just budding. I suffered great pain. As a result of my awareness and the inner work I was doing at the time I know this loss dragged me back not simply to my lost babies, but to my own premature birth. In the depths of despair and in the struggle to heal that loss, I wrote a poem entitled 'Benton'. It expresses the pain of premature loss.

> Benton lies buried in the soft womb that created him
> We rowed across
> My guide and I
> To the little island that would be his final resting place
> As we tenderly placed his little body in the bed
> That had been prepared for him
> You came to join us
> Together we watched as the tiny grave was filled
> Standing side by side we placed two daisies on his grave
> And said I love you
>
> Then you disappeared
> My tall blonde curly lover
> My quiet man
> You left as quietly as you had arrived
> The little boy we buried that evening
> Had blond curly hair
> And my brown eyes
>
> On the way across
> A bright golden light rose up from the tiny body
> I held in my lap
> It rose and rose and now shines down from the stars
> But it is also in the olearia bush by the gable of my home
> It is wherever I call it into being
>
> Goodbye my Benton
> Goodbye my quiet man.

In this poem I created an ideal. I did not kill off my lover in a fit of rage and pain as I might have done. I let him live in the airy realms of my dreams and my imagination so that I could speak to him whenever I wanted to. Although I did not realise it then, I had preserved him in my heart as someone I could find in the future. In the poem, I buried the child that symbolised our relationship, but I immortalised the love ideal. This meant that though I mourned the death of the heart, I kept love alive. I did not shut down. This was my way of healing my soul wound and it enabled me to move forward in my life and to dare to love again.

Whatever way we seek to express our grief, we must do so in order to heal the heart and to move on. The method I chose was writing. Or rather, it was writing that chose me! Something in me knew that this love had not been completed and it took time for me to heal. Expressing what was in my soul was very much part of the healing process. My lover was immortalised in my poetry. In my writing I gave birth to the creative spark in me that had been ignited by our love affair.

Mourning is a process and it cannot be rushed. The body heals in it's own time and so does the soul. The important thing is to dare to go to that place of hurt in the first place instead of clamming up and hoping that the pain will disappear. Time heals, and the pain of hurt eases. It is always important to express the feelings involved in loss however. People express their feelings in many different ways. Some will resolve their feelings of loss alone. Others will seek out another person to confide in. Writing, painting, working with one's dreams, drawing or simply working in the garden or walking in nature, all these methods work. The most important thing is to follow the dictates of the soul and to listen to its voice.

Reclaiming our inner feminine means having the willingness to suffer our heart wounds. If we do not take up the challenge to suffer and to heal the death of the heart, then at a deep level we cease to live. To dare to be lovers in a time of broken heart is all that is necessary to keep the heart open. The heart that loves is always young. It may be a sad and battle scarred heart that guides us to healing, but it is also a wise heart. Having experienced life with its ups and downs, pains and joys, we can move forward armed with the wisdom of the heart.

Notes

1.   C. O' Connor, My Father's Footsteps in *Changing Fathers* ed. Mc Keown

CHAPTER TEN

RECOVERING THE INNER KING

'The noblest of Kings holds the heart of the Weakest safe inside..'

(From Kings Don't Cry)

During difficult times in our lives when we experience painful and turbulent emotions, we often lose hope and fall into despair. We imagine that we will never resolve what is causing us pain, and we lose our belief in ourselves. At those times, we lose touch with our inner king. When we start to feel strong again and to believe that we can resolve our difficulties, we are recovering our inner king.

Trying to recover the inner king when our hearts are ravaged by loss is very difficult. Had I tried to begin writing this chapter yesterday for example, I would have got no further than the first line. Depressed and disillusioned, I had ceased for a moment to believe that my inner king existed. Instead my mind housed a fallen man, dejected and humiliated. Preoccupied and overburdened, I imagined I was incapable of completing my task. I was for a moment, daunted.

We all have times when we lose touch with our strength and abilities. We cease to believe in the inner king when we encounter obstacles and imagine ourselves defeated by these and when we lose hope that our dreams will be realised. Devastated, our king lies in ruins. He is a broken man, disappointed and disillusioned.

Our inner king is an archetypal male energy that exists in us all. It is a positive aspect of our animus, our inner man.

Like our animus it is innately present in us but is given form through our relationship with, and impressions of our personal fathers. As children we seek to emulate our parents particularly if we have a positive view of them. Often a father (or mother) will remain a strong positive figure in a person's life well after childhood and will be revered. If on the other hand, our childhood experience has been negative and we have felt hurt and let down by our father, then we will have difficulty resurrecting our own inner king. This will happen especially if we have perceived our father as disempowered in some way.

To experience a weak or emasculated father is particularly poignant for a boy since his father is his role model. If a boy looks up to his father and perceives him to be strong, capable and resourceful, this helps him develop these qualities in himself. As an adult he will be able to call on his inner king when he needs to be strong and in command of his life. In me, for example, the inner king represents my strength and my belief in my abilities to strive for what I believe in. When I am in touch with that strong part of myself then I can overcome obstacles in my life or blocks to my creativity and move on.

There is an outer dimension to the inner king. I wrote about this earlier in the book. There exists a collective image of the King, usually embodied in religions and myths and in contemporary life by public figures, heads of State and other leaders. These figures inspire us; we place in them our values and our aspirations and we look to them to lead us. Nowadays, traditional structures are no longer able to contain us as they used to, and in a time of change we seek the stabilising and grounding energy of a strong Group Father. The turning upside down of traditional values together with the enormous changes that are happening in the world means that we are often without meaning or purpose. We seek to find balance and stability. The Group Father's function is to hold us and to guide us when we have lost our way, just as the individual father's role is to guide the child into negotiating the world outside.

If there is a great sense of lack such as a collective and individual loss of soul, then the longing becomes too great to be contained in one person. Bly addresses this when he writes of the Death of the King in a time of no Father. He writes 'In a time when the Group Father has fallen, we approach the Sacred King and the Inner King with tremendous longing'.[1]

This longing at a soul level builds up in us a kind of idealism that can be difficult to live up to. Such idealism will be at great odds with the reality of our lives, so that there is a greater gap between our reality and our ideal. Our dreams appear totally out of our reach and we may believe that we can never achieve our goals. We lose the courage to pursue our destiny and follow in our soul's path.

We turn outside of ourselves to find inspiration when we lack self belief. In turning to the outer king we look to leaders or public figures to provide us with what we have lost inside. We seek direction. Public figures become icons carrying our collective ideals for us. An example of a female figure was Marilyn Monroe. She became an icon of the erotic and desirable feminine. A more recent example was Princess Diana who carried something of the collective wounded feminine. In the realm of the father we have Mahatma Gandhi, Martin Luther King, Nelson Mandela and many others.

Father hunger expresses itself as an intensified need for inspiration, direction and guidance. It means we over idealise and expect too much; we lose touch with the human aspect because we are blinded by our image of God and what we want to become or achieve. Being human becomes unbearable because it is not enough. There is then a great gap between God and us, or between reality and our idealism. We get depressed and begin to believe that we can never achieve our destiny, we can never follow our soul's path, and we are stuck with what is. And what is is then destined to disappoint us. We have nothing to look up to.

HUMANISING THE ARCHETYPE

Since the collective affects the personal, if there is a great lack of father in collective consciousness, then a lot is projected onto individual fathers. We look at our own fathers and we are disappointed. They seem small and insignificant and far too slight to fit the king's robes we want to dress them in. We forget that we are mortals and that every individual father is primarily a human being. At some point though, we have to accept our father for what he is. This in essence is part of growing up.

In developmental terms, the child grows away from his

father and his mother as he develops his own individual ego. He has to begin to see his parents as both fallible and capable of disappointing him. Accepting his father's limitations is necessary so that he can begin to form his own individuality. When a child does this, then he moves out of the Garden of Eden, he grows up. It means that over time, through repeated exposure to his parents in day to day living, he learns to humanise the archetype. He makes the Godlike figure of the parental imago into a human being with flaws and limitations. He learns that his father is human and can fail him. In adult psychological thinking, it means seeing the vulnerabilities involved in being human and recognising or sensing the child inside the king.

Joe's father left him and the family when he was still a small boy. Joe, like his brother, was devastated. Feeling rejected and abandoned, he believed his father no longer loved him. Many years later he learnt to understand his father as the product of his own upbringing and experiences, and so to humanise him. Seeing and appreciating his father's vulnerabilities meant that he was able to forgive him for the hurts he had experienced from him as a child. Having experienced his father as remote and unapproachable, as a young adult he was able to perceive his father differently and so to approach him. Accepting his father's limitations meant that he could begin to let go of his hurt and resentment at his father. To do this was a painful process, it meant that Joe had to connect with his own inner father and grow into his own individuality as a man. He had to find his own strength. When he did so he was able to stand outside the familial bonds that kept him tied in a place of unconsciousness, and to see himself as separate.

When we find and connect with our inner king then we can do this. Part of the process necessarily involves acceptance of the way things were and are. Acceptance frees up the energy otherwise caught up in trying to change the past. If Joe had remained consumed with anger and resentment at his father for having abandoned him, then he would have been unable to move on. This being said, acknowledging and releasing those hurt feelings is part of the process of change. There is no short cut to growth.

INTEGRATING
THE INNER CHILD INSIDE THE KING

Psychologically speaking, inside everyone are a King, a Queen, and a child. As adults, it is often hard for us to admit and allow our inner child into consciousness, usually because we are ashamed of him or her. Our inner child will awaken and clamour for attention when life events and relationships trigger old wounds. He or she will enter our lives uninvited and influence our feelings, actions and behaviour. The wounded child inside us is awakened particularly in intimate relationships. Unresolved childhood feelings, particularly if they are denied, can wreak havoc when we are relating closely to another.

In my experience, it is often particularly hard for a man to admit his inner wounded child into his consciousness. Ashamed by what he perceives as the child's greed and neediness when he as an adult man should be strong, he will seek to shut him away or at least quieten him. Many men shut the door firmly on their inner child because of fears that he will not be accepted. Identified with the prevailing attitude that men must be strong and not show their weaknesses, allowing his inner child into conscious awareness would expose a man and dent his confident persona.

James kept his wounded child well hidden. But as his relationship with Isabel deepened, the hurt and damaged boy inside him emerged more and more strongly and more and more often. Terrified of the greed and neediness of his spoilt inner child, he lashed out at Isabel. She was the only one who could take it; instinctively he knew this, for he felt safe with her. James was not consciously aware enough to realise why this was so. He had never been intimate enough with anyone before to let his child out. What he did not realise was that he damaged their relationship a little more every time. Each outburst created big black holes in their energy and tore the harmony of their lives apart. His unjustified anger pulled at the fabric of their relationship and sent Isabel into a place of reactive anger and then despair.

James's anger was unjustified because it was levelled at the wrong person. Disempowered, lonely and emotionally deprived as a child, James was taking it all out on Isabel. She understood it, but it hurt and paralysed her; she was power-less to prevent or circumvent it. She was familiar with James' moods that could turn him very quickly into what she termed 'his majesty the baby'. When in the grip of this energy, James became demanding and unreasonable and stamped his feet. He would set up situations he knew would upset her and when she protested, he would flare up into a rage. She was criticis-ing him, preventing him from doing what he wished to do and so forth. And 'why could she not accept him as he was?' This had become a stock phrase of his. Isabel knew it and despaired of it. She usually sensed these scenes well before they came. She tried to circumvent them by not reacting, and for a while succeeded. Inevitably however, she too fell into the pit of rage and destruction dragged up by their respective pasts. Her own reactions, guided by her inner child, ensured that she joined him and they were both lost. So the negative pattern of blame and reprisal rolled on. It took its toll on their relationship.

Isabel's inner child was equally wounded, but she expressed herself differently. In rows with James she became tearful and angry. Her vulnerability in loving him meant that she would do almost anything to keep him, and so she would respond to his coldness and anger by coaxing him back to her instead of distancing herself. He would threaten to leave. He often did leave, and Isabel feared this more than anything in the world. Isabel's inner child had a very great fear of aban-donment and this compromised her for it turned her into a hurt woman too fearful of rejection to stand up for herself. It meant that she lost her inner king to the wounded child. She lost her perspective on things. Her personal boundaries became blurred and she would compromise herself over and over again by accepting his behaviour. She allowed him to treat her badly by staying around rather than distancing her-self.

This kind of a pattern created a co-dependency in their relationship that was unhealthy. As in all relationships of this nature, awareness and willingness on both sides to work on their respective unresolved childhood behaviour patterns was necessary to break this co-dependency. Awareness however, is not always easy. It is far easier to remain unconscious. And in intimate relationships in particular, there is always the tendency to project onto the other and to fall into mutual complexes. When we are complexed, we are powerless in the grip of infantile feelings and behaviour. To pull ourselves out and become consciously aware of what is happening, we must connect with our inner king. Recovering the inner king for Isabel meant that she could walk away from James's rages and look after herself. It meant that the strong part of her could come to the fore to maintain her boundaries and hold and comfort the fearful and rejected child.

Recovering the inner king means integrating the child inside. It is not always easy to do this because it means acknowledging our vulnerability. Many years ago, involved with a man in whom I had quite consciously projected King, I wrote this poem. I called it *Kings don't cry*.

As you drove out of the drive
And I watched your car edge away from my home
My heart was full
I saw my King march forward defiant
But your noble head was bowed
Inside you carried a tiny child
Through your strength I sensed your weakness
Your sadness, Your loss
Noble as always in defeat
The tiny child in you was crying
Big tears of pain
I cried for you
I wanted to hold you in my arms
I wanted to soothe your brow

But Kings don't cry

I wanted to tell you
That I love your tiny child
And that the noblest of Kings holds the heart of the
weakest
Safe inside
I wanted to tell you that you are all the more noble to
me
In your nakedness
The crying child in you
Makes you the king that you are

And does not diminish the majesty of your love
Or the power of your passion

I know you left to hide your shame
You left because the King in you
Was tired of trying to keep the child at bay
You left because you were afraid I would turn away
When the King crumbled to the crying child
       For Kings don't cry

Most of us are ashamed of our wounds and of the child-ish part of us. Despite a great deal of inner work, our relating exposed this man's wounded child. Our relationship stirred up his vulnerabilities and the patterns of his childhood. His inner wounded child came to the surface at those times when he needed me and did not get what he wanted. Those were the times when I imagine I became, symbolically, his rejecting and depriving mother. Usually he would deal with his hurt by leaving. Staying would have been too painful and he was not yet prepared to meet that challenge.

Perhaps I was able to see his inner child and to have compassion for him because I was working on my own. When I felt devastated by his failure to meet my needs or his frequent absences, I had to take myself in hand. I had no choice. Ultimately there is no one person who can meet our needs. We must meet our own needs. I learnt this and I allowed myself to grow. First I had to accept my inner child for what she was. She was and still can be, wounded, angry, and also inclined to despair. She is lonely, and when she does not get what she wants, then she can become desperate and lose her sense of herself. I know that this little girl in me craves love above all else and because she does not always see too clearly she travels down the wrong roads for it and she gets lost.

I think men often find it hard to accept their wounded child because in relationship it opens their hearts and leaves them very vulnerable. It makes them feel ashamed. Having an emotionally needy inner child does not sit well on the shoulders of most contemporary men. It is still widely considered unacceptable for a man to express his deeper feelings, to cry and to express despair. As I have said earlier, there is less of a place to go when the inner child comes. Some men have got so used to disowning or rationalising their feelings that they do not even recognise the child when it appears. And also there is the cultural conditioning that men are the stronger sex and must protect the female. I believe these ancient archetypal images of male and female to be primed in us all, adding to the difficulties for many modern men in recognising and dealing with their vulnerabilities.

Brian taught me a lot about working with the inner child. Brian was a man in his forties, a very successful businessman who housed a lonely, terrified inner child. He led such a busy life that he had scant time to listen to the plaintiff cry of his inner child. He had great difficulty maintaining relationships, and had been in therapy for quite some considerable time. He told me that he carried a photograph of himself as a child in his pocket. He took it out during a session and showed it to me. I saw a lovely blond boy of eight or nine, who seemed lost and lonely. Brian told me that every evening he took the photograph out of his pocket and spoke to it. If he had had a long day and had been too busy to spend much time talking to the boy, he apologised for having neglected him. I was very moved by this and saw that Brian was healing his inner child in his way. Recovering the inner king means allowing the child to be healed by the father.

For women too, I believe it is very important to reclaim our inner king. He is the one who will hold us when we rage against our lovers for not getting what we want. He is the one who will hold us in a time of pain and despair. He is the one ultimately, when the crying is done, who will bring us back out into the world again. He is the one we have forgotten about because we generally project him onto our lovers, our men. He helps us to be assertive and to stand up for ourselves. He helps us believe in ourselves and restores our self-esteem when it has taken a battering. Just as the anima/Queen/ feminine principle in the man will lead him to his connection with his inner world and his feelings, so the animus/King /male principle in a woman will rescue her from the blackness of the forest and take her back out into the world.

James and Isabel's relationship was in trouble. James was grappling with his inner feminine, which, in her negative aspect, appeared as a dragon witch. She prevented him from doing what he wished to do. She called him selfish and a glutton, a coward and a bastard. He was not good enough; he was a lazy, good for nothing. Isabel could not find her inner king;

instead he was a broken, disillusioned man, weak and ineffective. James saw Isabel as a dragon witch and a needy child, she saw him as not only a greedy baby, but also a fallen king. Both needed to recover their respective inner kings. If James had connected with his inner king he would have been able to pacify his dragon, or he would have slain the dragon and banished the witch. He would have felt stronger in himself and more grounded in his centre. He would have felt less compelled to blame Isabel for everything that made him feel uncomfortable in his life. And if Isabel had connected with her own inner king she would have been able to stand back from James and not allow him to treat her badly. She would have held her own and looked after her own needs rather than projecting them onto James. She would have been less emotionally needy and dependent. Isabel's inner king would help her stand up to the enemies of her past and the negative energies and patterns that prevented her from moving on. Stronger, she would have been less of a prey to the demands and thrashings of James's wounded and majestic baby!

All this is to say that in order to recover the inner king we have to incorporate our vulnerability so that we look after ourselves. In spiritual language, it means taking our spirit back. Every time we project our needs onto another and make them responsible for us, then we give away our spirit. We lose something or all of ourselves, we become disempowered. Then we feel fragmented, disconnected and unwell. Our soul hates fragmentation and will always seek wholeness. This is what Jung called Individuation, the psyche's journey into wholeness. Taking our spirit back and connecting with our own essence is vital to healing our wounds.

THE INNER
MARRIAGE AND RELATIONSHIPS

In psychological terminology there exists what Jung called 'the Inner Marriage'. This really means the union of the opposites within the psyche of each person. When the King and the Queen, the male and the female principle are united within us, we are in balance. This is the kind of wholeness that our soul seeks. When we mend the split within, then we find peace, and our relationships can be harmonious. There is male and female energy in all of us. Often we forget this, as we tend to project our opposite onto our partners in a literal 'marriage' or union. And women fall in love with, and form partnerships with men who embody their 'animus' projection, just as men do with women who carry or embody their anima projection. This is natural, and part of the way in which our souls seek wholeness, union with another. However, it is widely known that one cannot maintain a healthy relationship with a partner unless one has a healthy relationship with oneself. The old cliché of not being able to love another unless one loves oneself is profoundly true. Wholeness begins at home, just as charity begins at home!

Each of us has male and female energy. These energies are different. One is active and generally projected outwards; one is receptive and often focussed more on being rather than doing. There are times when one or other energy is called for, and times when they need to operate in balance. In childbirth for example, a strange reversal of roles happens. The father is called upon to be in his feminine, receptive energy. We saw this in the examples I gave earlier in the book. It was highlighted symbolically during the event I talked about where I was giving a lecture as part of my book launch and my partner stood by and supported me. Likewise, when a mother is in the throes of childbirth, she is in her male active energy, although she is involved in a deeply instinctual female event. She is bringing the child into the world physically, and she is actively labouring. The father by contrast is not active, he waits and encourages, he loves and is open, and he supports with his presence.

Perhaps then the father present at the birth of his child

is giving birth to him or her spiritually, just as the mother gives birth physically. Thinking of the father's role in this way adds value and reverence to what being a father during pre-natal life and birth is all about. It adds another dimension to fathering and to the spirituality of childbirth. Instinctively, I feel this is an area that is only just opening up and that merits further work.

Relationships, particularly intimate relationships offer us a unique opportunity for growth and individuation. In relating to the other we see ourselves relating to ourselves. The other holds a mirror up for us. In an outer marriage we seek inner union. Intimate relationships initiate us into ourselves, they shape our lives and they reveal ourselves to ourselves. I mean this in the sense that in relating, we always unconsciously project aspects of our own personality on to the other. This is particularly so in intimate partnerships. This is why one's spouse is often referred to as 'the other half'! Rarely is the truth of that statement recognised. The other dynamic that happens when a couple begin to relate intimately is that in adapting to each other's personality one often mirrors the adaptations we made to our parents, teachers and other authority figures.

Isabel for example, in her relating to James, began to behave as a child in relation to a potentially abandoning par-ent. Her pattern was always to compromise herself because of her fear of abandonment. When things were not going well in her relationship with James, she was particularly inclined to lose herself, to abandon herself to him and to expect him to save her. This he felt as suffocating, and it pushed him even further into his area of vulnerability, which was a fear of inad-equacy and failure that rendered him angry and controlling. In contrast to Isabel, James had been overindulged as a child and had to fight for his own individuality. However, in close relationships he tended to unconsciously project the need to be looked after. He expected always to come first and to have everything on his own terms. When Isabel did not comply, he would become furious. When each was complexed in this way, then they related to each other from the past and as wound-ed children. They were not relating as adult James and Isabel.

Isabel's dream expresses how she lost and abandoned herself to James.

I am in a car with James. He is driving very fast; we a r e on the road to Sorrento in the South of Italy. It is a cliff road, very dangerous. I am scared and distressed and I ask him to slow down. He is shouting at me, arguing. I am leaning toward him in the car, as my car door is broken and will not shut. I have to keep it shut by holding it tightly with a string. He is driving very recklessly and I am very frightened that my door will open and I will fall out onto the road. He pushes me away roughly and I fall out onto the road. I awake in a sweat, in great fear.

Isabel had this dream when she and James were on holidays and were going through a difficult time. He was cold and aloof and pushed Isabel away. She was desperate to get close to him, but the more she did so, the more he became hard and distant. He was trying to make it clear to her that he could not meet her needs. He was also saying that he did not want the kind of intimate relationship she wanted. James hated intimacy, because it placed demands on him that he could not, or would not meet. Isabel's dream indicated how she abandoned herself, her safety to James. In the dream he is in control, he is driving. She has no protection as her door is broken and he is driving too fast. The dream indicated that in abandoning herself in that way to James, she was placing herself in great danger. It was a call from her soul to pull back and to look after herself and her own needs. In the dream James is also abusive to her and she is totally at the mercy of his anger. He is pushing her out of the car and symbolically the relationship.

Isabel had projected large chunks of herself onto James, most particularly her strength, and her inner king. She expected him to look after her. Of course, it is completely understandable that in close relationships we open to the other, and to an extent that we expect them to fulfil our needs. There has to be a certain give and take, otherwise there would be no real point in relating closely. Our partners fulfil our need for companionship, and physical and emotional love. However, often we are let down, and recognising the limitations of our partner is part of taking back our projections and having a healthier relationship. Also of course, recovering our own strength allows us to maintain our boundaries in relationship and to protect ourselves from unreasonable or hurt-ful behaviour.

Likewise, James' dream shows us very clearly the inner workings of his soul wound, that of a great anxiety and belief in his own inadequacy. James' dream came at a time when Isabel and he were having talks and arguments about the future of their relationship. As their relationship deepened, Isabel voiced a desire for a closer and more committed rela-tionship with the possibility of living together. James had responded with alarm and said he did not feel ready for that degree of commitment. After an argument, James had the fol-lowing dream.

I am at a car show. Mr. R is showing my friend and myself his taxis. There is a yellow taxi and another red one on a trailer. Although they are very beautiful, I think these are useless, because I know that they have fake bonnets and no engine. They are just for show. They don't work. Mr R. is proudly showing us the leather seats, the interior of the cars, which are beautifully finished. I think it is all a waste of time. There is a child there. There are also two girls present in the background and my friend M. is trying to get me to notice them. People are cleaning up, picking papers up off the floor. There is hardly anyone there because the event is over.

James dream shows us very clearly how perceptive he was about his own situation and the workings of his inner world. Being a very literal man however, he had great difficul-ty recognising the value of dreams and the unconscious life of the soul in general. In telling me about it, he identified with the beautiful cars, part of his heritage, but he also knew that there was a fake bonnet. Underneath there was no engine. In other words, the cars were fake. They were useless, and only there for show. His dream indicated that at some level he was aware of the inadequacy and shallowness of his personality. He felt himself to be fake. James was identified with his per-sona, with the result that he felt powerless and a sham. In effect, James did not feel adequate in himself as a man to be a full partner to Isabel. How could he offer her a commitment when he feared failing her, when he did not feel strong enough even to look after himself? James' inner king was certainly not alive at that particular time. Indeed in a throwaway remark he would say to Isabel that he was 'a broken man'.

Recovering the inner king then means taking back

aspects of ourselves that we have lost to the other in part-nership. This is not easy to do and may take a long time after the break-up of a relationship. We are almost always uncon-scious of the fact that we project parts of ourselves onto oth-ers, and so it may be hard to see what it is that we need to take back. I believe this psychological mixing of expectations and projections is why there are very often great feelings of anger and resentment at the ending of relationships. Mostly this is projected symbolically onto joint assets, house or prop-erty, and also more poignantly, children. The couple creates children jointly, and each parent will have parts of themselves invested in them. Disentangling these projections is all part of the process of separation. A slowness in letting go, and a reluctance to come to a place of closure after the ending of the relationship, is an indication that the person has not yet taken back their projections, or aspects of themselves they have placed in the other. They have not truly separated.

THE MIRROR WITHOUT

To understand the concept of projection in intimate rela-tionships one must think of a mirror. The other is a mirror of what we are oneself, but of which we are as yet, unaware of. Or more specifically, we see in the other aspects of our per-sonalities that we have not yet activated, or that are in poten-tial. We also project shadow onto others, and this accounts for people we don't like or have an irritation with. We generally repress our shadow, but if we draw that person we don't like into our lives, it is for a purpose. The purpose may not always be clear to us but nonetheless there is one. That person may reflect something that we need to become aware of in our-selves. If we attract a suspicious person into our lives for example, it is to get us to look at that side of our nature, or it can be a challenge to become more discerning. If we continu-ally attract the same sort of person into our lives, it is telling us that there is something we need to learn. Again our soul has a way of pulling us towards what most needs healing in our lives in order for us to become complete. As I said earlier, in relating to another, especially intimately, we are relating to an aspect of ourselves. This happens I believe, so that we will gain an understanding of our natures.

Georgina complained that she could never find a man who would commit to her. A vibrant career orientated woman in her mid forties, she had ended her marriage to a wealthy stockbroker because she felt trapped and confined by the constraints of marriage. She had two children, now in their late teens. Since the break-up of her marriage, she had had several relationships with men, but they always ended after a time, when it appeared she wanted 'more'. The men would not make the final commitment to her. She railed against them, and wondered why it was just her luck to fall for one Peter Pan after another.

'Have you thought that perhaps you are not ready to commit fully to a relationship yourself?' I queried. 'That's nonsense' she replied indignant that I should suggest such a thing.

Georgie had been coming to therapy regularly, and had committed herself to our weekly sessions. Although she was strong and articulate, and very successful in her career as a journalist, in many ways she seemed like an adolescent. Obsessed with the need to succeed in the outer world, she did not wish to be dependent on a man, yet a part of her craved intimacy. The call of nature pulled at her heart, the call of all women and men at some stage in their lives. She wanted to love and be loved but yet she also feared it. She was attractive and bubbly and had no difficulty meeting men. At some level though she frightened them. She was so successful, competent and together that she appeared to have everything a woman could want. What could they possibly offer her?

Typically, she chose men who were gentle and tender, and less successful in the outer world than she appeared to be. They were generally charming, attractive, creative types, who, when it came down to it, had great difficulty making a firm commitment. They appeared to mirror her need for independence. Possessed of a tender heart, she opened herself to love, and usually fell head over heels in love with her partners. She would abandon herself to her lovers, throw herself at their feet and then wonder why they hesitated. Invariably she was disappointed. Her partners then became hole-in-the -heart lovers, inadequate when they could not fulfil her needs. She felt hurt and rejected.

The irony of her story was lost on her. She had initially found a man who had committed himself to her totally, her former husband, but at that time she had wanted to get away. She felt confined. Georgina's soul pulled her to a different place, she sought freedom; she wanted to play. At some level therefore, she attracted men who were playmates, who also wanted to play. Perhaps they were all seeking freedom from the unresolved constraints of their childhood.

How we experience life whilst we are still forming our characters and dependent on our parents, will shape how we are as adults. A strongly activated Puer or Peter Pan energy in a personality indicates that there is a part of that person that did not feel free to play when a child. Or who felt thwarted or restricted in some way. Or it can mean that childhood was so idyllic that, like Peter Pan, the person does not want to grow up. In relationships if this energy is strong in one or other partner, it means that person has great difficulty growing up and taking responsibility for their actions and behaviour. Such a person will not want to be accountable in any way that might restrict their freedom. This fear of restriction often transmits itself as a failure or a reluctance to commit to another person.

Georgina's dilemma is not uncommon. She wants to root herself with a male partner, and yet a small part of her is not ready to do so or fears commitment to another and what that entails. Consciously she seeks union, but unconsciously the story is different and so her soul is telling her this by pulling her towards men who are at some level unavailable.

RECOVERING THE INNER KING

This Peter Pan energy is not exclusive to men who cannot grow up. Women may also have it. I recognise the *Puella* in myself. Puella is a Jungian term for the feminine version of the Puer or the Peter Pan. It is that part of us that seeks freedom in order to grow. It represents our free spirit. In that sense it has both a positive and a negative charge. The positive side is that it represents creativity and the ability to follow one's dreams and aspirations. It helps us to break and transcend boundaries. When the negative aspect is constellated however, it represents difficulties in growing up, accepting reality and necessary limitations.

The Father, or the King energy, is very much at the other end of the spectrum. Sometimes known in Jungian terminology as the Senex, he functions as a limiting, but also a stabilising or grounding factor. In times of chaos or instability, the King restores order and balance. Collectively as we have seen, he is very important at the moment. This is what reconnecting with the father means. It means recovering our strength and belief in our integrity and ourselves.

When Georgina is able to integrate her own king then she will stop seeking it in another. In a strange sort of way, when she starts to make a commitment to herself and to her needs, then she will attract a man at the same level who is finally able to commit to her.

As women, in order to achieve inner balance we must recover our own inner king and project less onto the men in our lives. When we have integrated our inner masculine and feminine, then we achieve the inner marriage. This means not only that we will be more in harmony with our essential natures, but also we will enjoy more fulfilling relationships. For men the task is the same. Either way, we need to take responsibility for recognising and meeting our own needs. Recovering the inner king ensures that we are capable of doing so.

I think many of us can satisfy our father hunger and our need for guidance through reclaiming our souls and developing our innate spirituality. Pursuing a spiritual path does not necessarily mean a religion. It means a commitment to finding the answers within rather than outside of us. It means turning inwards to find the essence and body of our souls. For some this is best done alone, but I believe it can also be done in relationship. The therapeutic relationship for example, is one place where the inner marriage is actively pursued through the natural process of individuation. And intimate relationships, especially when engaged in consciously, are great places to learn and to grow. In the vicissitudes and the ebb and flow of relating to another, we learn about all sides of human nature. We learn about compromise, about difference, and about the joy and pain of loving.

When Isabel finally learnt to walk away from James's infantile rages, she began to grow. When she learnt that she could distance herself from him without threat to her own security, she began healing her inner child. Isabel grew up when her inner king took her by the hand and led her out of that place of childhood where she had been compromised because of her insecurity. Because she had a great fear of abandonment, Isabel had allowed her inner child to pull her back to James when she should have been asserting herself and moving away from him.

Something similar has to happen for James. When he learns to pull back and to take responsibility for his actions and his feelings, he has a chance to become more solid and trustworthy. By recovering his inner king, by connecting with the father within, he will learn that he has the strength to care for, and fight for his own needs, without impinging on that of others. When he allows himself to be accountable and to accept the restrictions inherent to responsible adult life, James will go a long way towards healing his childhood wounds and taking his place in the world of men. Even though he is approaching middle age, in order to empower himself, he still requires the discipline of a strong internal father, something he lacked externally as a child. He needs a guiding hand to help him negotiate the world in a way that leaves him strong and capable. He needs to understand that he does not have to obey the dictates of his inner world at the expense of other people. When James connects in a very real way with his inner king, and the vacuum left by his dead father is filled by his own flesh and blood, he will emerge strong and fully a man.

James is still struggling to recover his inner King. In many ways, he is still searching for his father. Daunted perhaps by the challenges involved in deep psychological work, he left therapy before Isabel did. He began to withdraw more and more, not just from the therapeutic process, but also from the relationship with Isabel and ultimately, from himself.

He and Isabel split up after a long struggle with forces that they were unable to overcome. Their relationship did not negotiate the great changes that their meeting and their union stirred up in their lives. It was James who gave up first. Unaccustomed to the great surges of feeling that relating at this level meant, he forced Isabel out through repeated unreasonable and hurtful behaviour. Isabel, the more romantic of the two, struggled to keep them alive for as long as she could, until, heartbroken, she finally left him.

Isabel struggled to recover her inner king. Without James, though nursing yet again a wounded heart, she grew. Despite the pain she felt, over time she became stronger. She became more creative. In the space left vacant by James, she discovered herself. Though losing James pulled at her heart, her suffering honed her, forming her in a unique way. It was as though her love and loss gave her wings. Her soul soared with the wings of her love. She attended to her own work with the attention she had previously given to James. She wrote, and in her writing she gave birth to a part of herself she had not even known existed. Isabel recovered her inner king.

1.   R. Bly, *The Hunger for the King*.in *Fathers/Mothers* (ed). P.Berry (1991) p.16

©Benig Mauger

BIBLIOGRAPHY

Ackerman, R. *Silent Sons* Simon & Schuster, 1994

Berry, P. Ed. *Mothers/Fathers* Spring Publications, 1991

Biller, H. *Fatherhood: Implications for Child and Adult Development* in Wolman, B.(ed).*Handbook of Development Psychology* Prentice-Hall, 1982

Brazelton, T. *The Earliest Relationship* Karnac Books. 1991

Bly, R. *Father and Son* in Wilmer,H.(ed). Mother/Father Chiron, 1990

Bly, R. *The Hunger for the King in a Time with No Father* in.Berry,P. (ed) *Mothers, Fathers,* Spring, 1991

Bowlby, J. *Attachment and Loss* Vols.1&2 Hogarth Press, 1973

Chamberlain, D. *Babies Remember Birth* Ballantine Books, 1988

Cooper, D. *The Power of Inner Peace* Piatkus Books, 1994

Corneau, G. *Absent Fathers, Lost Sons* Shambhala, 1991

Correia,I.B. *The impact of television stimuli on the prenatal infant.* PHD Dissertation, Univ.New Sth Wales, Sydney, Australia (1994)

Coward, R. *Our Treacherous Hearts* Faber & Faber, 1993

De Casper,A.et al. Fetal reactions to recurrent maternal speech. *Infant Behaviour and Development,* 17 (2), 159-164

Desteian,J. C*oming Together-Coming Apart: The Union of Opposites in Love Relationships* Sigo Press, 1989

Erickson, E. *Childhood and Society* Norton, 19963

Ferguson, H.,McKeown,K.,Rooney,D. *Changing Fathers* Collins, 1998

Holmes,J. *John Bowlby and Attachment Theory* Routledge, 1993,

Hyde T. (ed) *Fathers and Sons* Wolfhound, 1966

Illich, I. *Limits to Medicine* Penguin 1988

Ianniruberto,A.et al. Ultrasonographic study of fetal *movements Seminars in Perinatology,* 5 (2) 175-181 (1981)

Jacobson, B. et al. Obstetric pain medication and eventual adult amphetamine addiction in offspring. *Acta Obstetrica Gynecologica Scandinavica,* 67,677-682 (1988)

Jacobson, B.et al. Opiate addiction in adult offspring through pos sible imprinting after obstretic treatment. *British Medical* Jrn.301,1067-1070 (1990)

Johnson, R.A. *The Fisher King & The Handless Maiden* Harper Collins, 1993

Jung, C.G. *Collected Works* (ed).Fordham et al. Bollingen Series XX 2nd edition 1967,reprint 1990

Jung, C.G. *The Significance of the Father in the Destiny of the Individual* CW4 paras 301-323, first published in 1909,revised 1949

Jung, C.G. *Memories, Dreams, Reflections* Fontana Press,1961

Jung, E. *Animus and Anima* Spring Publications, 1957

Keen, S. *Fire in the Belly: On being a Man* Bantam Books, 1991

Lewis, D.O.et al. Violent juvenile delinquents, Psychiatric, neurological, psychological, and abuse factors. *J.Amer.Academy Child Psychiatry,*18307-319 (1979)

Litt, S.M. *Perinatal Complications and Criminality.* Dissertation, Univ. Michigan, (1971)

Mauger, B. *Songs from the Womb-Healing the Wounded Mother* Collins Press, 1998

Mc Neely, D. *Mercury Rising: Women, Evil and the Trickster Gods* Spring Publications, 1996

Meade, M. *Men and the water of Life:Initiation and the Tempering of Life* Harper-Collins, 1993

Monick,E. *Phallos* Inner City Books, 1987

Moore, T. *Care of the Soul* Harper Collins 1992

Myss, C. *Anatomy of the Spirit* Bantam Books, 1996

Olivier, C. *Jocasta's Children* Routledge, 1989

Piontelli, A. *From Fetus to Child* Routledge, 1992

Samuels, A.(ed). *The Father, Contemporary Jungian Perspectives* Free Association Books, 1985

Shinoda-Bolen, J. *Crossing to Avalon* Harper Collins, 1994

Shinoda-Bolen, J. *Gods in Everyman* Harper Collins, 1984

Williams, N. *As it is in Heaven* Picador, 1999

Wilmer, H. Ed. *Mother Father* Chiron publications,1990

Verney, T. *The Secret Life of the Unborn Child* Sphere Books, 1982

Stern, D. *The Interpersonal World of the Infant* Basic Books, 1985

Stevens, A. *The Two Million-Year-Old-Self* Texas A&M University Press, 1993

Von Franz M.L. *Projection and Recollection in Jungian Psychology* Open Court, 1980

Vincent Priya, J. *Birth Traditions and Modern Pregnancy Care* Element Books, 1992

Winnicott, D.W. *The Maturational Process and the Facilitating Environment* Hogarth Press, 1965 *Through Paediatrics to Psychoanalysis*, Hogarth Press,1965

Zukov, G. *The Seat of the Soul* Rider, 1991